T0128336

BUDDHIST YOGA

BUDDHIST YOGA

A Comprehensive Course

Translated by THOMAS CLEARY

SHAMBHALA
Boston & London
1995

SHAMBHALA PUBLICATIONS, INC.
Horticultural Hall
300 Massachusetts Avenue
Boston, Massachusetts 02115
www.shambhala.com

Printed in the United States of America

Distributed in the United States by Random House, Inc.,
and in Canada by Random House of Canada Ltd

LIBRARY OF CONGRESS CATALOGING-IN-PUBLICATION DATA

Tripiṭaka. Sūtrapiṭaka. Saṃdhinirmocanasūtra.
  English. Buddhist yoga: a comprehensive course/translated by
  Thomas Cleary.
    —1st ed. p. cm.
  ISBN 1-57062-018-0
  I. Cleary, Thomas.
BQ2092.E5C54 1995   94-46663
294.3'85—dc20   CIP

BVG 01

CONTENTS

TRANSLATOR'S PREFACE

The word *yoga* has many meanings, including the ideas of union, method, effort, and meditation. The elaborate psychophysical exercise routines of Hindu Yoga are familiar to Westerners, but the subtle metaphysics and refined methods of spiritual development characteristic of Buddhist Yoga are not well known.

This volume presents a translation of the *Sandhinirmochana-sutra*, "Scripture Unlocking the Mysteries," a complete classical sourcebook of Buddhist Yoga. This is one of the main texts of that stream of Buddhist tradition known as Vijnanavada, "The Doctrine of Consciousness," or Yogachara, "The Practice of Yoga."

This sutra, or scripture, provides a remarkably detailed course in the philosophical and pragmatic bases of Buddhist Yoga. This is a text that is meant to be read and reread many times as essential preparation by those who are thinking of undertaking meditation exercises of any sort. This procedure was the classical way, and many of the shortcomings and aberrations of modern Western meditation cults can be traced to abandonment of this tradition.

The *Sandhinirmochana-sutra* is divided into eight sections, including an introduction in the classical style. As in the case of all universalist Buddhist scriptures, the introduction to this text is an important part of the work, making preliminary presentations of key principles and practices in a highly concentrated setting, partly symbolic and partly literal.

The second section of the sutra, entitled "Characteristics of Ultimate Truth," opens with a discussion of the nonduality of all things. This is taken to mean that phenomena are in essence neither "created" nor "uncreated," neither mundane nor supernal. Concluding that the real nature of things is beyond words, the discussion goes on to depict ultimate truth as inaccessible to thought and deliberation, beyond all objects, beyond all forms, beyond all representation, beyond all controversy. For the purposes of Buddhist Yoga, therefore, it is essential to understand that ultimate reality is not a philosophical construct.

The sutra then goes on to discuss the relationship between ultimate truth and practices. Through an extensive course of reason based on the logic of metaphysics and corresponding spiritual experience, the point is established that ultimate truth and practices are neither one and the same nor completely different. This is an essential insight, one that distinguishes the special nature of Buddhist Yoga; it is based on one of the most important reforms initiated by Gautama Buddha in the spiritual practices of ancient yoga.

This discussion is followed by descriptions of intellectual and spiritual conceit consequent upon failure to perceive the ultimate truth pervading all things. The entire section is then closed with the logical conclusion that all-pervasive ultimate truth is everywhere one and has no differentiation in itself in spite of pervading all differentiations. To see the integrity of ultimate truth underlying the fragmented facade of ordinary experience is one of the purposes of Buddhist Yoga.

The third section of the sutra's course outlines working descriptions of mind, intellect, and consciousness. Here are found the classical Buddhist psychological constructs of eight and nine consciousnesses, which are used as a basis of orientation in yoga. This brief section of the sutra concludes with a transcendental description of mastery of these mysteries as a state of consciousness in which, by virtue of focus on ultimate truth, there is no inner discrimination of, or identification with, phenomena corresponding to constructed definitions.

The fourth section of the sutra deals with the general characteristics of all phenomena; their conceptualized, dependent, and perfectly real characteristics. The conceptualized characteristic of things refers to phenomena as we conceive of them and speak of them. The dependent characteristic of things refers to interdependent origination of phenomena, which thus exist only as part of universal relativity and not as individually self-subsistent entities. The perfectly real characteristic of things refers to *thusness,* the direct experience of phenomena without the superimposition of conceptual descriptions.

Pragmatic understanding of the distinctions among these three characteristics is essential to correct practice of Buddhist Yoga and correct realization of emptiness, without which there is no possibility of spiritual liberation. This section on the characteristics of all phenomena is thus followed up in the next section by a discussion of essencelessness, the Buddhist principle of emptiness.

Here, essencelessness is defined in three ways. First is essencelessness of characteristics, which refers to the nature of conceptualized characteristics projected on phenomena. Second is essencelessness of birth, which refers to the dependent or relative character of phenomena, which by virtue of their interdependence have no individual point of origin. Third is ultimate essencelessness, referring to the selflessness of all things, which is called the ultimate truth.

The sutra emphasizes the critical importance of these realizations in the process of actualizing intellectual and spiritual liberation. Accordingly, after defining accurate understanding of essencelessness, the text goes on at length discussing the misunderstandings that typically arise, analyzing the origins and consequences of specific misapprehensions of Buddhist teachings on Emptiness. This section concludes with a recapitulation of three phases of Buddha's teaching, in which the principles of essencelessness are at first occult, then implicit, finally explicit. With understanding of the final explicit teaching, it is realized that ultimate truth actually pervades all the scriptures, even if at first in a covert manner; the teaching that brings this out is thus called a complete doctrine.

The sixth section of the sutra's course consist of an extraordinarily detailed discussion of the principles and practices of Buddhist yogic meditation. The procedures, problems, resolutions, and results of meditation are analyzed with great precision in this section, enabling the practitioner to avoid the pitfalls and hazards of ignorant or misguided concentration.

The seventh section of the course deals with the ten transcendent ways and ten stages of enlightenment, which are comprehensive outlines of Buddhist Yoga. The transcendent ways are practices by which one transcends the world while in its very midst. The teachings of the ten stages of enlightenment are called the Alphabet of Buddhism, the basic "letters" of meaning from which all utterances of Buddhist teaching are composed. This section of the sutra defines the transcendent ways and the stages, outlining their curative and developmental functions and effects. This section of the sutra should be read in conjunction with the *The Ten Stages* in the comprehensive Buddhist sutra known as *The Flower Ornament Scripture,*★ for an in-depth perspective on the transcendent ways and the stages in which they are practiced.

The final chapter of the sutra's course on Buddhist Yoga, entitled "Deeds of the Enlightened," presents a typically de-

---

★Thomas Cleary (trans.), *The Flower Ornament Scripture: A Translation of the Avatamsaka Sutra* (Boston and London: Shambhala Publications, 1993), book 26. In the earlier, three-volume edition of this work, book 26 is in volume 2 (1986).

tailed analysis of the qualities, capacities, and domains of operation that characterize a Buddha, or a fully enlightened mind.
Here the critical distinction is drawn between liberation and
enlightenment, the latter referring to the total sublimation and
completion of the individual. The completion is made possible
by liberation, but liberation alone does not of itself bring completion. Thus the scripture concludes the course with an inten-
sive recapitulation of the sphere of knowledge and action of the
enlightened.

1. INTRODUCTION

Thus have I heard. Once the Buddha was staying in a great palace, which was made of the finest jewel flowers, supremely brilliant, adorned with seven precious substances, radiating great light illumining all regions in all worlds, studded with beautiful ornaments.

The girth of the palace was boundless, immeasurable, beyond the range of the world. It was produced by supreme transmundane virtues, and its appearance was that of ultimately independent pure consciousness.

It was the capitol of the Buddha, the gathering place of great enlightening beings, with all kinds of other beings always in attendance. It was supported by the joy and bliss of the universal taste of truth. It appeared arrayed with adornments benefiting sentient beings in all suitable ways, getting rid of the binding defilement of all afflictions and driving away the evils of bedevilments.

It was the basis of the adornments of the enlightened. Its pathways were mindfulness and knowledge, its vehicles were great tranquillity and subtle observation. Its entrances were the great liberations of emptiness, signlessness, and wishlessness, and its adornments were infinite virtues.

With supremely pure awareness, the Buddha was attached neither to the mundane nor the supramundane. He proceeded according to formless truth and dwelt in the abode of the enlightened ones. He had arrived at equality with all the enlightened ones and had reached the point of nonobstruction and the state of unchangeability.

Unimpeded in all actions, the Buddha's devices were inconceivable. Roaming in the equality of past, present, and future, his being was in all worlds. He was free from doubt in cognition of all things and had accomplished great enlightenment in all actions, without confusion in knowledge of all truths.

The embodiments manifested by the Buddha were undifferentiable. His was the knowledge properly sought by all enlightening beings; he had attained the state of nonduality with all enlightened ones. His supreme transcendence was unadulterated; his enlightened liberation and subtle knowledge were consummate. He realized the boundless equanimity of Buddhahood, with no inside or out, comprehending the cosmos, throughout all space and time.

The Buddha was with a group of innumerable great disciples, who were well trained in all respects, each an heir of the Buddha. Their minds and intellects were liberated, their conduct was pure. They pursued the enjoyment of truth, learned a lot, retained what they learned, and their learning had accumulated.

These disciples considered well what they had to consider, explained well what they had to explain, and did well what they had to do. They had perfected the intellectual jewels of swiftness, keenness, the quality of being emancipating, discernment, breadth, and uniqueness; and they had attained higher knowledge.

All of these disciples had attained felicity in their present state, and were great pure fields of blessings. Their deportment was tranquil and mature in every respect, and they were most tolerant and gentle. They had already put the wise teaching of the Buddha into practice.

There were also countless great enlightening beings, who had come from various Buddha-lands. All of them were established in the great vehicle of universal enlightenment, practicing the teaching of the great vehicle. Their minds impartial toward all sentient beings, they were free from all discriminations, including discrimination between discrimination and nondiscrimination.

The enlightening beings overcame all bedevilment and opposition, and still they avoided the thoughts of those absorbed in individual salvation. Sustained by the vast joy and bliss of truth, they were beyond fears of ill repute, death, miserable states, and intimidation by groups. Proceeding directly into the stage of nonregression, they stopped the appearance of all calamities for all sentient beings.

The names of those enlightening beings were Unlocking the Implicit Intent of the Profound Doctrine, Profound Questioner, Offspring of the Teaching, Purified Intelligence, Vast Intelligence, Root of Virtue, Born of Ultimate Truth, Independent Seer, Benevolent One, Glorious One, and so on.

2. CHARACTERISTICS OF ULTIMATE TRUTH

At that time Logical Questioner, in the presence of the Buddha, asked Unlocking the Implicit Intent of the Profound Doctrine, "When it is said that all things are nondual, what are all things, and what is nonduality?"

Unlocking the Implicit Intent of the Profound Doctrine replied, "All things are generally of two kinds, created and uncreated. Of these, the created are neither created nor uncreated, and the uncreated too are neither uncreated nor created."

Logical Questioner asked further, "How is it that the created is neither created nor uncreated, and the uncreated is neither uncreated nor created?"

Unlocking the Implicit Intent of the Profound Doctrine replied, " 'Created' is an artificial definition temporarily set up by the Buddha. As such, it is a verbal expression assembled by conceptualization. If it is a verbal expression assembled by conceptualization, ultimately it is a verbal expression of various conceptualizations, and not actually real. Therefore it is not created.

"If you say it is uncreated, this too comes down to a matter of words. If you talk about anything outside of the created and the uncreated, the same thing applies.

"That does not mean, however, that there is nothing being discussed. What is that thing? Sages, with their knowledge and vision, detach from names and words, and therefore actualize enlightenment. Then, because they wish to make others aware of this nature that is beyond words, they temporarily set up names and characteristics and call something created.

" 'Uncreated' is also an artificial definition temporarily set up by the Buddha. As such, it is a verbal expression assembled by conceptualization, which means that it is ultimately verbal expression of various conceptualizations, and so is not actually real. Therefore it is not uncreated.

"If you say it is created, this too comes down to a matter of words. Even if you talk about anything outside of the created and the uncreated, the same thing applies.

"That does not mean, however, that there is nothing being discussed. What is the thing? Sages, with their knowledge and vision, detach from names and words, and therefore actualize enlightenment. Then, because they want to make others aware of this nature beyond words, they temporarily set up names and characteristics and call something uncreated."

Then Logical Questioner asked Unlocking the Implicit Intent of the Profound Doctrine, "What are these things that sages, having detached from names and words and thus realized enlightenment, provisionally characterize as 'created' and 'uncreated' in order to make others aware of this nature beyond words?"

Unlocking the Implicit Intent of the Profound Doctrine said, "Suppose a magician or his apprentice gathers a bunch of grass, leaves, wood, and pebbles at a crossroads, and produces magic effects, creating the appearance of elephants, horses, chariots, soldiers, jewels, conch shells, coral, stores of various goods and grain, and so on. Deluded, ignorant, stupid people, who do not know or understand anything, think that the magic effects of elephants and horses and so on, which they perceive produced in the grass, leaves, wood, and pebbles, are really there. They cling fast to what they perceive, and say that this alone is real and that all else is delusion. They still need to examine further.

"If people are not ignorant or dull-witted, if they are intelligent and perspicacious, when they see the magic effects they think that there are no real elephants and horses and so on in those magic illusions produced in the grass and leaves and wood and pebbles. They realize that the illusions deceive their eyes, producing various images. They do not cling to what they perceive as the only reality. In order to convey this point, they also make verbal explanations. They do not need to examine further.

"If people are ignorant and have not yet attained the transcendent wisdom of sages, and cannot comprehend the true nature of all things beyond words, then when they have seen or heard of the created or the uncreated, they think that there really must be a 'created' and an 'uncreated' in what they have apprehended. They cling to what they see and hear, and say that this alone is true and that all else is ignorant folly. They need to examine further.

"If people are not ignorant, and have seen the holy truths, and have attained the wisdom of sages, and know the true nature of all things beyond words as it really is, when they see or hear of the created and the uncreated they think that there really is no such thing as the created or the uncreated, but there are active forms created by discrimination, which are like magical effects deceiving the intellect into producing notions of created and uncreated, or notions of difference between created and uncreated. They do not cling to what they have seen or heard, or claim it is the only truth. In order to convey this point, they too make verbal explanations. They do not need to examine further.

"In this way, in the midst of these things, sages detach from names and words by knowledge and insight, and therefore real-

ize enlightenment. Then, because they want to make others
aware of this real nature which is beyond words, they provisionally set up names and characteristics and call things created
or uncreated."

Then, to restate this point, Unlocking the Implicit Intent of
the Profound Doctrine said in verse:

> Buddha explains the meaning of nonduality beyond words;
> It is most profound, beyond the scope of the ignorant.
> The ignorant, confused by delusion about this,
> Cling to duality and make false descriptions;
> They are either unsettled or fixed in error
> And revolve forever in the pains of birth and death.
> Still repudiating discourse on true knowledge like this,
> They will be reborn as goats and sheep.

Then the great enlightening being Offspring of the Teaching
said to the Buddha, "World Honored One, east of here, past as
many worlds as grains of sand in seventy-two Ganges Rivers, is
a world called Renowned. The Buddha there is called Great
Renown. I left that Buddha's land to come here.

"In that land, I once saw a place where there were seventy-
two thousand philosophers and their teachers, gathered together
in one assembly to consider the characteristics of the ultimate
meaning of things. As they thought and assessed and contemplated and searched all over together, they were after all unable
to get to the ultimate meaning of all things—just a medley of
different interpretations, conflicting interpretations, varying interpretations. They contradicted one another and argued, got
out weapons and attacked and wounded one another, finally
breaking up and going their separate ways.

"At that time, I thought to myself, 'The appearance of a Buddha in the world is most wonderful; because of the Buddha's
appearance in the world, it is possible to understand and realize

the ultimate truth that is beyond the scope of all thought and deliberation.' "

The Buddha said, "It is so. It is as you say. I have awakened to the ultimate truth, which is beyond all thought and reflection. And I explain it to others, revealing and analyzing it, defining and elucidating it. Why? The ultimate truth of which I speak is that which is inwardly realized by sages, while the scope of thought and deliberation is what unenlightened people testify to among themselves. Therefore, you should know that ultimate truth transcends all objects of thought and deliberation.

"The ultimate truth of which I speak has no form to which to relate, whereas thought and deliberation operate only in the sphere of form. Based on this principle, you should know that ultimate truth transcends all objects of thought and deliberation.

"The ultimate truth of which I speak cannot be expressed in words, whereas thought and deliberation operate only in the realm of words. Based on this principle, you should know that ultimate truth transcends all objects of thought and deliberation.

"The ultimate truth of which I speak has no representation, whereas thought and deliberation operate only in the realm of representation. For this reason, you should know that ultimate truth transcends all objects of thought and deliberation.

"The ultimate truth of which I speak puts an end to all controversy, whereas thought and deliberation operate only in the realm of controversy. For this reason, you should know that ultimate truth transcends all objects of thought and deliberation.

"A man accustomed to pungent and bitter flavors all his life cannot think of, or assess, or believe in the sweet taste of honey and sugar.

"Someone in ignorance who has an overwhelming interest in desires because of passionate craving, and is therefore inflamed with excitement, thus cannot think of, or assess, or believe in the marvelous bliss of detachment and inward effacement of all sense data.

"Someone in ignorance who clings to rhetoric because of an overwhelming interest in words, thus cannot think of, or assess, or believe in the pleasure of holy silence with inner tranquillity.

"Someone in ignorance who clings to the signs of the world because of overwhelming interest in perceptual and cognitive signs thus cannot think of, or assess, or believe in the ultimate nirvana that obliterates all signs so that reification ends.

"People in ignorance cling to mundane conventions because they have various controversies and beliefs involving attachments to self and possessions, and thus cannot think of, or assess, or believe in a utopia where there is no ego, no possession, no attachment, and no contention. In the same way, you should know, those who pursue thoughts cannot think of, or assess, or believe in the character of the ultimate truth that is beyond the sphere of all thought and deliberation."

Then, to restate this point, Buddha said in verse:

The inwardly realized signless sphere
Cannot be verbalized, having no expression.
The ultimate truth that stops all argument
Transcends all aspects of thought and deliberation.

Then the enlightening being Purified Intelligence said to the Buddha, "World Honored One, it is most wonderful how well you have explained this. The character of ultimate truth of which you speak is very subtle and profound, transcending the aspects of sameness and difference of all things, difficult to comprehend.

"Once I saw a group of enlightening beings, who were at that time cultivating the stage of zealous application, sitting together deliberating on the sameness or difference of the ultimate truth and practices. One party said that there is no difference at all between ultimate truth and practices. Another party said that it is not true that there is no difference at all between ultimate truth and practices, that ultimate truth is different from practices.

"Others were doubtful and hesitant; they said, 'Whose words are true, whose are false? Who is practicing correctly, who incorrectly?' Some called out, 'Ultimate truth and practices have no difference at all.' Others called out, 'Ultimate truth is different from practices.'

"Seeing them, I thought, 'These people are ignorant and dull. They are not illumined, not good, not practicing rightly, unable to understand that ultimate truth is so subtle and profound that it transcends sameness with and difference from practices.' "

The Buddha said, "It is as you say. They are ignorant and dull. They are not illumined, not good, not practicing rightly, unable to understand that ultimate truth is so subtle and profound that it transcends sameness with and difference from practices. Why? When one does practices as they do, one cannot be said to comprehend ultimate truth or to be able to realize it.

"Why? If ultimate truth and practices had no difference at all, everyone would already see the truth, and everyone would already have attained the highest expedient, tranquil nirvana, or they would have already attained supreme perfect enlightenment.

"If ultimate truth were totally different from practices, those who already see the truth would not do away with the forms of practices. If they did not do away with the forms of practices, they would be bound by forms and would not attain liberation; since those who see the truth would in that case be bound by forms and not liberated, furthermore, they would also not be liberated from crude bondage to the physical self. Because of not being liberated from these two kinds of bondage, those who have seen the truth would not be able to attain the highest expedient, tranquil nirvana, or realize supreme perfect enlightenment.

"But not everyone has seen the truth, not everyone has been able to attain the highest expedient, tranquil nirvana, and not everyone has realized supreme perfect enlightenment. Therefore it is not right to say that ultimate truth and practices are no different at all.

"It is not the case, furthermore, that those who see the truth are not able to do away with the forms of practices; and indeed they do dismiss them.

"And it is not the case that those who see the truth are unable to shed bondage to forms; and they are indeed liberated.

"And it is not the case that those who see the truth are unable to shed crude bondage to the physical self; and they are indeed liberated.

"Because they are able to shed these two kinds of bondage, they can also attain the highest expedient, tranquil nirvana; and some can realize supreme perfect enlightenment. So it is not right to say that ultimate truth and practices are totally different.

"If ultimate truth were no different from practices, then when practices degenerate into impurity, ultimate truth would also degenerate into impurity. If ultimate truth were totally different from practices, then it would not be true that the common characteristic of practices is ultimate truth. Now then, because ultimate truth does not degenerate into impurity, and because the common characteristic of practices is the characteristic of ultimate truth, it is not right to say either that ultimate truth is no different from practices or that ultimate truth is totally different from practices.

If ultimate truth were no different from practices, then just as the aspect of ultimate truth within practices has no differentiation, so also would the forms of practices have no differentiation; then whatever they see, whatever they hear, whatever they are aware of, and whatever they know, those who cultivate contemplative practices would not need to seek ultimate truth after that.

"If ultimate truth were totally different from practices, it would not be true that practices being just the manifestation of selflessness and absence of inherent nature is the characteristic of ultimate truth.

"Also, if practices and ultimate truth were totally different, they should simultaneously establish each other separately as defiled and pure.

"Now then, since the forms of practices actually do have differences and are not undifferentiated, then whatever they perceive, those who cultivate contemplation practices still need to seek ultimate truth.

"Furthermore, practices themselves being the manifestation of selflessness and absence of inherent nature is called the characteristic of ultimate truth.

"Also, it is not that defilement and purity simultaneously establish each other as separate.

"Therefore, it is not right to say either that ultimate truth and practices are no different or that they are completely different."

"The whiteness of a shell can hardly be defined either as one with or as distinct from the shell. The same is true of the goldenness of gold. The musicality of the sound of pipes can hardly be defined either as one with or as distinct from the sound of the pipes. The fragrance of incense can hardly be defined as either one with or as distinct from incense. The pungency of pepper can hardly be defined either as one with or as distinct from pepper. The softness of silk can hardly be defined either as one with or as distinct from silk. The cream in milk can hardly be defined either as one with or as distinct from milk. The impermanence of all actions, the misery of all contaminated states, and the selflessness of all phenomena can hardly be defined either as one with or as different from actions, contaminated states, and phenomena. The restlessness and impurity of craving can hardly be defined either as one with or as distinct from craving; the same is true of hatred and folly. In the same way, ultimate truth cannot be defined either as one with or as different from practices.

"I am truly aware of this characteristic of ultimate truth, which is very subtle, extremely subtle, very deep, extremely deep, difficult to comprehend, extremely difficult to comprehend, transcending the sameness and difference of things. Having realized it, furthermore, I explain it, reveal it, analyze it, define it, and clarify it for others."

Then the Buddha spoke a verse to restate this principle:

The realm of actions and ultimate truth are beyond
    sameness and difference;
Those who discriminate sameness and difference
    are not acting rightly.
People are bound by forms and gross materiality;
They should practice cessation and contemplation
    so as to attain release.

Then the Buddha said to the reverend Subhuti, "Do you know how many people are conceited and approve their understanding because they are possessed by conceit? Do you know how many are free from conceited notions of understanding?"

Subhuti replied, "I know there are few who are free from conceited approval of understanding. I know there are countlessly many who are conceited and approve their understanding because they are possessed by conceit.

"Once when I was staying in a forest, there were many mendicants also staying in that forest near me. I saw them separate into groups and explain various teachings according to the contemplations they had achieved, approving their understanding.

"One type approve their understanding because of having apprehended the physical and mental clusters, because of having apprehended the characteristics of the clusters, because of having apprehended the beginning of the clusters, because of having apprehended the ending of the clusters, because of having apprehended the extinction of the clusters, because of having apprehended the extinction of the clusters and made that their realization.

"Just as this type based their understanding on apprehending the clusters, another type based theirs on apprehending the sense media, another on apprehending conditional origination, in the same way. There was also another type who approved their understanding based on apprehending nourishment, the characteristics of nourishment, the beginning of nourishment, the end of nourishment, the extinction of nourishment, and taking the extinction of nourishment for realization.

"There was another type who approved their realization based on apprehending the truths, the characteristics of the truths, thorough knowledge of the truths, eternal detachment through the truths, taking the truths as realization, and attaining practice of the truths.

"There was another type who approved their understanding based on having apprehended the elements, the characteristics of the elements, the variety of the elements, the nonunity of the elements, the extinction of the elements, and taking extinction of the elements for realization.

"There was also another type who approved their understanding based on attaining the points of mindfulness, realizing the characteristics of the points of mindfulness, realizing what and how the points of mindfulness cure, achieving cultivation of the points of mindfulness, being able to produce those points

of mindfulness as yet undeveloped, and to strengthen, perpetu-
ate, and extend the points of mindfulness once they have been
developed.

"Just as there were those who based their understanding on
the points of mindfulness, there were also those who based
theirs on the right efforts, the bases of occult powers, the religious faculties, the religious powers, the branches of enlightenment. There were also those who approved their understanding
based on realizing the eightfold noble path, the characteristics
of the path, how and what the path cures, the practice of the
path, developing the path from scratch, and strengthening, per-
petuating, and extending the path.

"Seeing these mendicants, I thought to myself, 'These elders
expound various teachings based on the contemplations they
have realized, and approve their understanding. Obviously
these elders are all conceited. Because they are possessed by
conceit, furthermore, they are unable to understand the unity
of the ultimate truth that pervades all.

" 'Therefore Buddha is most marvelous, the Buddha explains
well, in that the Buddha says the character of the ultimate truth
is subtle, most subtle, profound, most profound, hard to comprehend, most hard to comprehend, and it pervades all appearances.' Even for the mendicants practicing Buddhism, it is hard
to comprehend the oneness of the ultimate truth pervading all;
how much more difficult for those on other paths!"

Then the Buddha said to Subhuti, "It is so, Subhuti, it is so.
I have truly awakened to the most subtle, most profound, most
difficult to comprehend, unique ultimate truth that pervades all.
Having realized it, furthermore, I explain, reveal, analyze, define, and bring it to light for others.

"How so? I have already pointed out that the pure object of
attention in all the body-mind clusters is ultimate truth. I have
already pointed out that the pure object of attention in all sense

media, conditional origination, nourishment, truths, elements, points of mindfulness, right efforts, bases of occult powers, religious faculties and powers, branches of enlightenment and branches of the path, is ultimate truth.

"This pure object of attention is uniform and undifferentiated in all the body-mind clusters, and also in all the sense media, and so on, including in the branches of the path. You should know, therefore, that ultimate truth is everywhere one.

"Subhuti, once practitioners of contemplation have penetrated the selflessness of phenomena in the absolute sense in true thusness in one cluster, they do not further seek the selflessness of phenomena in the absolute sense in true thusness individually in the other clusters, the sense media, conditional origination, nourishment, the truths, the points of mindfulness, the right efforts, the bases of occult powers, the religious faculties and powers, the branches of enlightenment and the branches of the path. Simply by following this nondual knowledge of ultimate truth of true thusness as the touchstone, they closely observe and proceed to realization of the uniform ultimate truth pervading all. Based on this principle, you should know that ultimate truth is everywhere one.

"Subhuti, the clusters are variously different. The sense media, conditional origination, nourishment, the truths, the elements, the points of mindfulness, the right efforts, the bases of occult powers, the religious faculties and powers, the branches of enlightenment, and the branches of the path, are also variously different. If the selflessness of phenomena in the ultimate sense in true thusness were likewise differentiated, then the selflessness of phenomena in the ultimate sense in true thusness would also have a cause and would be causally produced. If it were causally produced, it would be created; if it were created, it would not be ultimate truth. If it were not ultimate truth, it would be necessary to search further for another ultimate truth.

"Therefore, the selflessness of phenomena in the ultimate sense in true thusness is not said to have a cause, is not causally produced, is not created. This is ultimate truth. Having realized this ultimate truth, one no longer seeks any other ultimate truth. There is only the stability of the true nature of things, the abiding of the realm of reality, which is constant and perpetual whether or not Buddhas appear in the world.

"Based on this principle, Subhuti, you should know that ultimate truth is everywhere one. Just as the space in all kinds of different forms is signless, undifferentiated, unchanging, all-pervasive, and uniform, so is the ultimate truth within all things, which are different in nature and form, all-pervasive and uniform."

Then the Buddha recapitulated in verse:

This all-pervasive uniform ultimate truth
The Buddhas say has no differentiation.
Any who imagine difference therein
Are certainly ignorant and conceited.

3. CHARACTERISTICS OF MIND, INTELLECT, AND CONSCIOUSNESS

Then the enlightening being Vast Intelligence said to the Buddha, "You speak of enlightening beings who are versed in the mysteries of mind, intellect, and consciousness. What does this refer to, and how is such an enlightening being defined?"

The Buddha replied, "It is good that you are able to ask me about such a profound matter. You have asked this question because you want to aid and comfort innumerable beings, because you have compassion for the world and want to foster their welfare and happiness. Listen closely, and I will explain the meaning of the mysteries of the mind, intellect, and consciousness.

"You must know that in mundane life and death, the various creatures fall into various categories of beings. They may be born in various ways, and their bodily parts go through a process of development. In the course of this process, at first the mind and consciousness containing all potentialities develop, combine, and grow, based on two kinds of grasping. One is grasping the material organs of sense and what they are based on. The other is grasping the habit energy of false description expressing arbitrary conceptions of characteristics and names. These two kinds of grasping are present in the realm of form, but not in the formless realm.

"This consciousness is also called clinging consciousness, because this consciousness follows and clings in the body. It is also called repository consciousness, because this consciousness receives and stores in the body, indifferent to good or bad. This consciousness is also called mind, because this consciousness accumulates and increases form, sound, scent, flavor, feeling, and so on.

"With the clinging consciousness as the basis, the foundation, the bodies of six consciousnesses operate—the consciousness of the eye, ear, nose, tongue, body, and intellect. Here, the eye, consciousness, and form and color are the conditions producing eye-consciousness. Discriminating conceptual consciousness operates along with eye-consciousness, at the same time and with the same objects.

"The ear, nose, tongue, and body with consciousness, and sound, scent, flavor, and feeling, are the conditions producing ear-consciousness, nose-consciousness, tongue-consciousness, and body-consciousness. Discriminating conceptual consciousness operates along with these consciousnesses, at the same time and with the same objects.

"When the eye-consciousness alone is operating, there is only one discriminating conceptual consciousness operating along with the eye-consciousness. When two, three, four, or five bodies of consciousness are operating, there is still only one discriminating conceptual consciousness operating along with the five consciousness bodies.

"It is like a torrent of water: if conditions for the production of one wave appear, then only one wave is formed; if the conditions for the production of two or more waves appear, then two or more waves form. The torrent itself, nonetheless, flows constantly, without interruption of exhaustion.

"It is also like a clear mirror: if the conditions for one image are there, just one image appears; and if the conditions for two or more images are there, then two or more images appear. The surface of the mirror itself does not change into images, and no end to its function can be found.

"In the same way, because the torrentlike clinging consciousness acts as a basis, as a foundation, when there are conditions producing the eye-consciousness, then the eye-consciousness operates, and when there are conditions producing the five consciousness bodies, the five consciousness bodies operate.

"Even if enlightening beings are versed in the mysteries of mind, intellect, and consciousness based on knowledge of reality, nevertheless the Buddha does not consider them to be versed in all the mysteries of mind, intellect, and consciousness. If enlightening beings inwardly truly do not see clinging or clinging consciousness, do not see repository or repository consciousness, do not see accumulation, do not see mind, do not see the eye, form, or eye-consciousness, do not see ear, sound, or ear-consciousness, do not see nose, scent, or nose-consciousness, do not see tongue, flavor, or tongue-consciousness, do not see body, feeling, or body-consciousness, do not see intellect, phenomena, or conceptual consciousness, then they are called enlightening beings well versed in ultimate truth. The Buddha defines them as enlightening beings versed in ultimate truth; these are called enlightening beings versed in all the mysteries of mind, intellect, and consciousness."

Then the Buddha spoke a verse to restate this principle:

The clinging consciousness is very deep and subtle;
All potentials are like a torrential flow.
I do not explain this to the ignorant,
For fear they will get the idea it is self.

4. CHARACTERISTICS
OF ALL PHENOMENA

Then the enlightening being Root of Virtue said to the Buddha, "You speak of an enlightening being familiar with the characteristics of phenomena. To what does this refer, and how is such an enlightening being defined?"

The Buddha said, "It is good that you ask about this profound matter. You have asked this question because you want to aid and comfort innumerable beings, because you have compassion for the world and want to foster their welfare and happiness. Listen closely, and I will explain the characteristics of phenomena.

"Phenomena all have three kinds of characteristics. First is the characteristic of mere conceptual grasping. Second is the characteristic of dependent origination. Third is the perfect characteristic of reality.

"The merely conceptual characteristic of phenomena as grasped refers to the differences in the identities of things as provisionally defined by names in order to talk about them.

"The characteristic of dependent origination of phenomena means that the inherent nature of all things is dependent origination. When something exists, then something else exists; when something is produced, something else is produced. For example, ignorance conditions actions, and so on, ultimately bringing together a mass of suffering.

"The perfect characteristic of reality in phenomena is true

thusness, which is equal in all things. Enlightening beings can realize this true thusness by diligent effort, right attention, and unperverted thought. Realizing this, and gradually cultivating this realization, they will ultimately reach true enlightenment, and then witness it fully.

"The merely conceptual characteristic is like the affliction of a man with cataracts in his eyes. The characteristic of dependent origination is like the various optical illusions appearing to the man with cataracts. The perfect characteristic of reality is like the unconfused sphere of operation natural to clear eyes without cataracts.

"Suppose clear crystal is combined with blue coloring, with the result that it looks like sapphire; it confuses people, because they mistake it for sapphire. Combined with red coloring, it looks like ruby; it confuses people, because they mistake it for ruby. Combined with green coloring, it looks like emerald; it confuses people, because they mistake it for emerald. Combined with yellow coloring, it looks like gold; it confuses people, because they mistake it for real gold.

"The coloring agent on the crystal is like the habits of description held to by conceptualization imposed on dependent existence. The misapprehension of the crystal as sapphire, ruby, emerald, or gold is like clinging to conceptualization imposed on dependent existence. The clear crystal itself is like dependent existence. Just as the appearances of sapphire, ruby, emerald, or gold imposed on the crystal never have any reality, never have intrinsic being, the characteristics imposed on dependent existence by conceptual clinging never have any reality or intrinsic being. You should know the perfect characteristic of reality to be like this.

"The characteristic of conceptual grasping can be known through the association of names and characterizations. The characteristic of dependent origination can be known through the conceptual clinging superimposed on dependent existence. The perfect characteristic of reality can be known by not clinging to conceptions superimposed on dependent existence.

"If enlightening beings can truly know the characteristic of conceptual grasping superimposed on the dependency of phenomena, then they can truly know all phenomena as signless. If they truly know the characteristic of dependency, they can truly know all phenomena in their defiled aspect. If they truly know the perfect characteristic of reality, they can truly know all phenomena in their pure aspect. If enlightening beings truly know signlessness in dependency, then they can put an end to defilement; if they can put an end to defilement, they can realize purity.

"In this way, enlightening beings truly know the conceptualized, dependent, and real characteristics, they truly know signlessness, defilement, and purity. Because they truly know signlessness, they can cut off all defilement and therefore can realize all purity. These are called enlightening beings versed in the characteristics of phenomena; the Buddha defines them as such."

Then the Buddha spoke a verse to restate this principle:

If you do not know phenomena are signless,
You cannot eliminate their defilement.
When you do not eliminate defilement,
You ruin realization of subtle purity.
If you do not see the faults of conditionings,
Indulging conditionings, you will hurt living beings.
Negligent of the stable and the unstable,
Pitiful is the loss in missing one and reifying the other.

5. ESSENCELESSNESS

Then the enlightening being Born of Ultimate Truth said to the Buddha, "Once when I was staying alone in a quiet place, these reflections occurred to me: 'The Buddha has explained, in innumerable ways, the individual characteristics, characteristics of birth and death, resolution, and total knowledge, of the clusters, sense media, conditional origination, and nourishments.

" 'In innumerable ways, the Buddha has explained the individual characteristics, total knowledge, resolution, realization, and practice of the truths.

" 'In innumerable ways, the Buddha has explained the individual characteristics, variety, multiplicity, resolution, and total knowledge of the elements.

" 'In innumerable ways, the Buddha has explained the individual characteristics of the points of mindfulness, how and what they cure, how they are cultivated, how they are first produced, how they are perpetuated and developed.

" 'The Buddha has also explained all these aspects of the right efforts, bases of occult powers, religious faculties and powers, the branches of enlightenment, and the eightfold noble path.

" 'The Buddha also says that all things have no essence, no origin or extinction, that they are fundamentally quiescent and inherently nirvanic.'

"I wonder, what is the inner intent based on which you say all things have no essence, no origin or extinction, that they are fundamentally quiescent and inherently nirvanic? Please be so compassionate as to explain the hidden meaning of this."

The Buddha said, "Good, good! Your reflections are most reasonable. It is good that you are able to ask about this profound matter. You have asked this question because you want to aid and comfort innumerable beings, because you have compassion for the world and want to foster their welfare and happiness. Listen closely, and I will explain for you the inner intent of the saying that all things have no essence, have no origin or extinction, are fundamentally quiescent and inherently nirvanic.

"You should know that when I say all things have no essence, I am alluding their to three kinds of essencelessness: essencelessness of characteristics, essencelessness of birth, and ultimate essencelessness.

"What is the essencelessness of characteristics of all things? It is their conceptually grasped character. Why? Because the characteristics are defined by artificial names, not by inherent definition. Therefore this is called essencelessness of characteristics.

"What is the essencelessness of birth of things? It is the dependently originated character of things. Why? Because they exist dependent on the power of other conditions and do not exist of themselves. Therefore this is called essencelessness of birth.

"What is the ultimate essencelessness of things? It means that things are said to be essenceless because of the essencelessness of birth; that is to say, the fact of dependent origination is also called ultimate essencelessness. Why? I reveal the pure object of attention in things to be ultimate essencelessness. Dependency is not a pure object of attention, so I also call it ultimately essenceless.

"There is also the perfectly real character of things, which is also called ultimate essencelessness. Why? Because the selflessness of all things is called ultimate truth and can also be called essencelessness. This is the ultimate truth of all things and is revealed by essencelessness, so for these reasons it is called ultimate essencelessness.

"You should know that essencelessness of characteristics is like flowers in the sky. Essencelessness of birth is like illusory images, and so is ultimate essencelessness in part. Just as space is only revealed by absence of forms and yet is omnipresent, so also is one part of ultimate essencelessness, because it is revealed by the selflessness of things, and because it is omnipresent.

"It is in allusion to these three kinds of essencelessness that I say all things are essenceless. You should know that it is in allusion to the essencelessness of characteristics that I say all things have no origin or extinction, are fundamentally quiescent and inherently nirvanic.

"Why? If inherent characteristics of things have no existence at all, then they have no origination; if they have no origination, then they have no extinction. If they have no origination and no extinction, they are fundamentally quiescent. If they are fundamentally quiescent, they are inherently nirvanic, and there is nothing at all therein that can further cause their ultimate nirvana. Therefore I say that all things have no origination or extinction, are fundamentally quiescent and inherently nirvanic, in terms of the essencelessness of characteristics.

"I also allude to ultimate essencelessness revealed by the selflessness of things when I say that all things have no origination or extinction and are fundamentally quiescent and inherently nirvanic. Why? Because the ultimate essencelessness revealed by the selflessness of things is the eternal and constant real nature of all things, permanent and uncreated, having no relation to any defilements.

"Because the eternal and constant nature of things is permanent, it is uncreated. Because it is uncreated, it has no origination or extinction. Because it is unconnected to any defilements, it is fundamentally quiescent and inherently nirvanic. Therefore I say that all things have no origination or extinction, are fundamentally quiescent and inherently nirvanic, in terms of ultimate essencelessness revealed by the selflessness of things.

"Moreover, I do not define the three kinds of essencelessness because of taking various types of people's particular views of conceptualized essence as essence, or because of taking their particular views of dependent or real essences as essence. I define the three kinds of essencelessness because people add a conceptualized nature on top of the dependent nature and the real nature.

"People produce explanations of the dependent and real natures based on the characteristics of the conceptualized nature, saying they are such and such, in accord with how people conceptualize them. Because the explanations condition their minds, because their awareness conforms to the explanations, because they are lulled by the explanation, they cling to their conceptualizations of the dependent nature and real nature as such and so.

"Because they cling to their conceptualizations of the dependent and real natures, this condition produces the dependent nature of the future, and due to this condition people may be defiled by afflictions, actions, or birth, and forever rush around in repetitious cycles, with no rest, suffering pains and vexations, going through all kinds of psychological states.

"Furthermore, if people have never cultivated good, or cleared away mental obstructions, or matured their minds, or practiced much zealous mental application, or been able to accumulate virtue and knowledge, I explain things to them based on the essencelessness of birth.

"Once they have heard this, they are able, according to their capacity, to understand that all conditionally produced actions are impermanent, inconstant, unstable, and subject to change and disintegration. Then they become wary of conditioned acts and deeply disillusioned, whereupon they stop evils and are able to avoid doing evil things and to cultivate good practices diligently. Because of practicing what is good, they become able to cultivate good qualities, clear away mental obstructions, and develop consistency, whereby they practice much zealous application and accumulate much virtue and knowledge.

"Even though they cultivate good and accumulate virtue and knowledge in this way, however, they are nevertheless as yet unable to truly know the essencelessness of characteristics and the two kinds of ultimate essencelessness in essencelessness of birth. So they cannot yet truly be disaffected with all conditioned actions and are not yet truly detached from desire or yet truly liberated. They are not yet totally liberated from the defilements of afflictions, they are not yet totally liberated from the defilements of actions, and they are not yet totally liberated from the defilements of birth.

"The Buddha goes on to explain more essential principles to them, namely the essencelessness of characteristics and ultimate essencelessness, in order to enable them to be truly disaffected with all conditioned acts, so that they can be truly free from desire and truly liberated, so that they can transcend all defilements of afflictions, actions, and birth.

"Once they have heard this teaching, they are able to truly believe in the essencelessness of characteristics and ultimate essencelessness in the essencelessness of birth, and to investigate and contemplate these and realize them in truth, so as to be able to not cling to conceptualized nature in the dependent nature.

"Because of knowledge that is not conditioned by words, not thinking in conformity with words, free from the lull of words, they are able to extinguish dependency. Sustained by the power of knowledge in the present state, they are able to extinguish the causes of the future.

"Because of this, they are able to be truly disaffected with all conditioned acts, able to truly detach from desire, able to truly become liberated, able to become totally liberated from the threefold defilement of afflictions, action, and birth.

"People with the temperament for the vehicle of sainthood also realize unexcelled peaceful nirvana by way of this path, this course of practice. People with the temperament for the vehicle of self-enlightenment and people with the temperament for the vehicle of universal enlightenment also realize unexcelled peaceful nirvana by way of this path, this course of practice. All saints, self-enlightened ones, and enlightening beings share this one marvelous pure path. All have this one ultimate purity in common; there is no second. It is in this sense that I say there is only one vehicle.

"It is not that there are not various types of people. Some people are dull, some are mediocre, some are sharp. If people have the temperament and personality of disciples who only seek tranquil sainthood, then even if they are taught the various methods of vigorous practice set up by the Buddha, that could not, after all, enable them to sit on the site of enlightenment and realize supreme perfect enlightenment. Why? Because they basically only have a lesser nature, their compassion is slight, and they just fear suffering.

"Because their compassion is slight, they give up on working for the benefit of the many. Because they fear suffering, they give up on undertaking various activities. I never would say that those who wholly give up working for the benefit of the many, and who wholly give up undertaking various activities, will sit on the site of enlightenment and realize supreme perfect enlightenment. That is why I call them disciples who only seek tranquillity.

"As for persons with the temperament for sainthood who are dedicated to enlightenment, I also call them enlightening beings in another respect. Why? Having become liberated from the barriers caused by afflictions, when they are inspired by Buddhas, their minds can also attain liberation from the barriers of knowledge. Because they first cultivate practices for their own benefit, in order to become liberated from the barriers caused by afflictions, the Buddha defines them as being of the temperament of disciples seeking sainthood.

"In this way, furthermore, various differences can be found in people's understandings of my well-explained, well-ordered teaching, good doctrines explained with the purest intent. Based on these three kinds of essencelessness, by deeply hidden allusion, in the scriptures of incomplete doctrine the Buddha explains the essential principles—that all things are essenceless, have no origination or extinction, and are fundamentally quiescent and nirvanic—in hidden, secret forms.

"As regards this scripture, if people have cultivated superior good, have cleared away obstructions, have developed consistency, and have practiced much zealous application, but have not yet been able to accumulate stores of superior virtue and knowledge, and yet are simple and direct, even though they do not have power to think discerningly and to discard and affirm, still they do not dwell fixed in attachment to their own views.

"If they hear such a teaching as this, even though they do not have the power to truly understand my profound esoteric speech, nevertheless they are able to develop interest in this teaching and develop pure faith, believing that this scripture is the word of Buddha, that its profound revelation is connected with profound emptiness, hard to see, hard to understand, impossible to pursue in thought, not in the realm of thought and deliberation, subtle and refined, to be understood by those with brilliant knowledge.

"In reference to the doctrines expounded in this scripture, they slight themselves and persist in talk like this: 'The enlightenment of the Buddhas is most profound. The true nature of all things is also most profound. Only Buddhas can properly understand; it is incomprehensible to people like us. The Buddhas turn the wheel of right teaching for people of various interests; the Buddhas have measureless knowledge and vision, whereas our knowledge and vision is like the hoof track of an ox.'

"Although they are able to respect this scripture, relate it to others, copy it, keep it, read it, disseminate it, honor it, receive it, recite it, and memorize it, nevertheless they are as yet unable to apply its mode of practice, and therefore cannot comprehend the words I speak with a most profound hidden meaning. Under these conditions, the people still can increase their stores of virtue and knowledge, and after that, those who have not developed consistency can do so.

"If people have not yet been able to accumulate stores of superior virtue and knowledge, and are not simple and direct by nature, and still persist in clinging to their own views even though they have the power to think discerningly and to discard and affirm, when they hear such a teaching, they are unable to truly understand what I say with hidden intent. Even if they believe in such a teaching, they make a rigid literal interpretation of the meaning, saying that all things definitely have no essence, definitely are not originated or extinguished, definitely are fundamentally quiescent, and definitely are inherently nirvanic. Because of this, they acquire a view of nothingness, or a view of nonexistence of characteristics, in regard to all things.

"Because they get the idea of nothingness, or the idea of nonexistence of characteristics, they deny all characteristics, saying they are nonexistent; they deny the characteristic of mere conceptualization, the characteristic of dependence, and the real characteristic of all things.

"Why? Since the conceptualized characteristic can only be

set up if the dependent and real characteristics exist, as long as one sees the dependent and real as nonexistent, one also denies conceptualized characteristics. Therefore I say they deny all three characteristics.

"Although they think my teaching is right, still the meaning is not what they think it is. Because they think my teaching is right and yet impute wrong meaning to it, they hold on to the teaching as right and hold on to the wrong meaning. Although their virtue may increase because of belief in the teaching, nevertheless they lose wisdom because they cling to the wrong meaning. Because of the loss of wisdom, they lose innumerable good qualities.

"Also, other people hear from them that the teaching is right and that it has this meaning, which is in fact not the meaning. If they follow their views, they will think of this teaching as right, but will impute the wrong meaning to it. They will hold to the teaching as right but will hold to the wrong meaning, and will therefore also lose good qualities.

"If people do not follow their views, and upon suddenly hearing from them that all things are essenceless, unoriginated and imperishable, fundamentally quiescent and inherently nirvanic, become frightened and claim that these are not the words of the Buddha but of the devil, they will repudiate and vilify this scripture, and as a result will suffer great loss and run into great behavioral obstruction. For this reason, I say that to see all characteristics as absent and proclaim a false doctrine is the way to create a massive behavioral obstruction, because those who do so bring about the downfall of innumerable good people and cause them to have great behavioral obstruction.

"If people have not cultivated good, have not cleared away obstructions, have not developed consistency, have not much zeal, have not accumulated stores of virtue and knowledge, are not straightforward, and persist in clinging to their own views even if they have the power of discernment and choice, when they hear such a teaching as this, they cannot truly understand what I say with a deep secret meaning, and they do not believe in this teaching. They think this teaching is wrong, they think the meaning is not the meaning, and they cling to these views.

"They claim this is not the word of the Buddha but of the devil, and with this idea they repudiate and vilify this scripture, discard it as false, and destroy and refute it in innumerable ways, considering those who believe in it to be their enemies. They are already obstructed by their behavior, and because of that are now further obstructed by this behavior. This behavioral obstruction is easily set up at first, but eventually there is no prospect of getting out of it for millions of eons.

"Thus, such differences can be found in people's interpretations of my well-explained, well-ordered teaching, good doctrines explained with the purest intent."

Then the Buddha spoke these verses to recapitulate:

All things are essenceless,
Birthless, deathless, fundamentally still;
All things are inherently nirvana.
Who with wisdom would say there is no hidden meaning?

The characteristics, birth, and ultimate truth of things are
    essenceless;
This I have now revealed.
Those who do not know this hidden meaning of the Buddha
Lose the right path and cannot go on it.

The pure who rely on the pure paths
Rely only on this—there is no second.
While I therefore define it as one vehicle,
It is not that people are not different.

Countless people in the world of the living
Only save themselves by heading for tranquillity;

Rare are the valiant who realize nirvana
Yet do not abandon other beings.

In the subtle, inconceivable realm of noncontamination
Liberation is equal, without distinctions;
All meaning is realized, confusion and suffering are shed.
In other words, it is called permanence and bliss.

Then the enlightening being Born of Ultimate Truth said to
the Buddha, "What the Buddhas say with hidden meaning is
most wonderful, subtle, profound, hard to comprehend. As I
understand what the Buddha has said, in the midst of transient
appearances on which are based the conceptualized characteristics that are the sphere of discrimination, if one artificially labels
a definition as, for example, the cluster of matter, whether in
terms of inherent characteristics or distinguishing characteristics,
and artificially labels definitions as the birth of the cluster of
matter, the extinction of the cluster of matter, the eternal over-
coming of the total knowledge of the cluster of matter, whether
in terms of inherent characteristics or distinguishing characteristics, this is called conceptualized characterization. The Buddha
defines the essencelessness of characteristics on this basis.

"As for the transient appearances themselves, on which are
based the conceptualized characteristics that are the sphere of
discrimination, they are called dependent characteristics. The
Buddha defines the essencelessness of birth of things, and one
part of ultimate essencelessness, on this basis.

"This is the way I now understand the meaning of what the
Buddha says. Inasmuch as the conceptualized characteristics in
the transient appearances on which are based the conceptualizations that are the sphere of discrimination are not actually true,
therefore this inherent essencelessness, true thusness in which
phenomena have no identity, the pure focus of attention, is
called ultimate reality. The Buddha defines part of ultimate essencelessness on this basis.

"As the foregoing applies to the cluster of matter, so also does it apply to the other clusters, the twelve sense media, the twelve elements of becoming, the four kinds of nourishment, and the eighteen elements.

"As I understand the Buddha's meaning, in the transient appearances on which are based the conceptual characteristics that are the sphere of discrimination, if one artificially labels definitions 'the truth of suffering,' or 'complete knowledge of the truth of suffering,' whether in terms of inherent characteristics or distinguishing characteristics, these are called conceptualized characteristics. The Buddha defines the essencelessness of characteristics on this basis.

"The transient appearances themselves on which are based the conceptualized characteristics that are the sphere of discrimination are called dependent characteristics. The Buddha defines the essencelessness of birth of things, and part of ultimate essencelessness, on this basis.

"As I understand the Buddha's meaning, inasmuch as the conceptualized characteristics in the transient appearances on which are based the conceptualizations that are the sphere of discrimination are not actually true, this inherent essencelessness, true thusness in which things have no identity, the pure focus of attention, is called ultimate reality. The Buddha defines part of ultimate essencelessness on this basis.

"As this applies to the 'truth of suffering,' so also does it apply to the other truths. And as it applies to the noble truths, so also does it apply to each of the points of mindfulness, the right efforts, the bases of occult powers, the religious faculties and powers, the elements of enlightenment, and the elements of the path to enlightenment.

"Just as an efficacious ingredient must be put into all medicines, in the same way this definitive teaching of essencelessness—that all things have no inherent identity, have no origin or destruction, and are fundamentally quiescent and inherently nirvanic—permeates all of the scriptures of incomplete doctrines; it must be in all of them.

"Just as the background of a painting is the same throughout the work of painting, whatever colors are used, and it furthermore makes the paintwork clear, in the same way this definitive teaching of essencelessness permeates all the scriptures of incomplete doctrine, the same in every case, and can also make the incomplete doctrines in those scriptures clear.

"Just as sweet filling put inside cakes produces an even finer flavor, in the same way this definitive teaching of essencelessness, put into all the scriptures of incomplete doctrines, produces greater joy.

"Just as space is all-pervasive, the same everywhere, and does not obstruct any activities, in the same way this definitive teaching of essencelessness pervades all the scriptures of incomplete doctrine and is the same everywhere, and yet does not obstruct the practices cultivated by all disciples, the self-illuminated, and enlightening beings."

Then, praising the enlightening being Born of Ultimate Truth, the Buddha said, "Very good. You have ably explained the meaning of the words of profound intent spoken by the Buddha, and you have ably constructed similes, saying it is like an effective ingredient in medicine, like the background wash of a painting, like the sweet filling in a cake, like space pervading everywhere. Yes indeed, this is how it is. This is how you should understand and remember it."

Then, Born of Ultimate Truth went on to say to the Buddha, "In the beginning, the Buddha just taught the four noble truths, for those inclined to the vehicle of disciples. Although this was very rare and marvelous, and no one had been able to teach this before, there was still something beyond that teaching, some room; it was incomplete, and it was a ground of controversies.

"In the second phase, for those inclined to practice the great vehicle, the Buddha taught that all things are essenceless, without origin or destruction, fundamentally quiescent, and inherently nirvanic; but the Buddha taught this in a covert, implicit manner. Although this was even more marvelous, yet there was still something beyond the teaching of that period, still some room; it was still incomplete, still a ground of controversies.

"Now in this third period, for all those aiming for the great vehicle, the Buddha openly and explicitly teaches the essencelessness of all things, that all things have no inherent identity, no beginning or end, are fundamentally quiescent and inherently nirvanic. This is most marvelous; there is nothing beyond it, no more room for doubt. This is the true complete teaching, in which controversy has no foothold.

"If good men and women, having heard the Buddha's profound complete teaching that all things are void of intrinsic essence, have no origin or destruction, are fundamentally quiescent and inherently nirvanic, believe in it with understanding, write and copy it, preserve it, honor it, circulate it, learn it and reiterate it, become thoroughly familiar with it, reflect on it reasonably, and put it into practice, how much merit will they produce?"

The Buddha said, "The merit produced by these good men and women would be immeasurable, hard to know, but I will briefly tell you a little. Just as the amount of earth one could place on one's nail scarcely amounts to the smallest imaginable fraction of the whole earth, and the amount of water in the hoofprint of an ox scarcely amounts to the smallest imaginable fraction of the amount of water in the oceans, in the same way the merit gained by believing and practicing the scriptures of incomplete doctrines scarcely amounts to the smallest imaginable fraction of the merit developed by believing and practicing the teaching of this scripture of complete doctrine."

Then, Born of Ultimate Truth said to the Buddha, "What should this teaching unlocking mysteries be called, and how should it be upheld?"

The Buddha said, "This is called the complete teaching of ultimate truth. You should uphold this complete teaching of ultimate truth."

When this complete teaching of ultimate truth was spoken, six hundred thousand people in the audience became determined to realize supreme perfect enlightenment. Three hundred thousand listeners became detached from the data of sense, were freed from defilement, and attained clarity of objective vision of all things. One hundred and fifty thousand listeners put a final end to all contaminations, and their minds were liberated. Seventy-five thousand enlightening beings attained acceptance of nonorigination.

6. ANALYZING YOGA

Then the enlightening being Maitreya said to the Buddha, "Based on what, abiding in what, do enlightening beings practice tranquillity and observation in the great vehicle?

The Buddha replied, "You should know that the basis and abode of practice of tranquillity and observation in the great vehicle are the provisional setups of the ways of enlightening beings, and sustaining the determination for supreme perfect enlightenment."

Maitreya then asked, "The Buddha has said that there are four kinds of objects. One is reflections of thought. The second is reflection of nonthought. The third is the totality of all phenomena. The fourth is practical accomplishment. How many of these four are objects of focus in tranquillity, how many are objects of focus in observation, and how many are objects of focus in both tranquillity and observation?"

The Buddha replied, "One, that which is without conceptual images, is the object of focus in tranquillity. One, that which has conceptual images, is the object of focus in observation. Two, the totality of phenomena and the accomplishment of tasks, are objects of focus in both tranquillity and observation."

Maitreya asked, "How can enlightening beings seek tranquillity and perfect observation based on these four kinds of objects?"

The Buddha said, "Enlightening beings listen carefully to the teachings I have devised for them, assimilate them, become familiar with them, reflect on them, and arrive at insight into them. Then, in solitude, they attentively meditate on these principles for careful reflection. Then they attentively meditate on the inner stream of the meditating consciousness. When they practice correctly in this way, they are very calm and stable, giving rise to physical and mental ease. This is called tranquillity. This is how enlightening beings can seek tranquillity.

"By attainment of physical and mental ease as a basis, in respect to the images on which the concentration within those useful contemplations focuses intently, they observe mental forms, attain higher understanding, and become detached. Then they are able to correctly discern the knowable meanings of the images of concentration, to discern them to the fullest possible extent, to thoroughly ponder and investigate them. Involving recognition, appreciation, precise awareness, vision, and contemplation, this is called observation. This is how enlightening beings can perfect observation."

Maitreya went on, "If enlightening beings focus on the mind as object and inwardly meditate on the mind, but have not yet attained physical and mental ease, what should their exercise of attention be called?"

The Buddha said, "This is not the attention of tranquillity. It is attention involved in application to tranquillity."

Maitreya asked, "If enlightening beings have not yet attained physical and mental ease, what about the attentive meditation on the images focused on in concentration on the principles being contemplated—what should this attention be called?"

The Buddha said, "It is not the attention of observation. It is attention involved in application to observation."

Maitreya also asked the Buddha, "Should the path of tranquillity and the path of observation be said to be different, or to have no difference?"

The Buddha replied, "They should be said to be neither different nor not different. Why are they not different? Because the object of concentration in observation is mind. Why are they not without difference? Because differentiated images are not the focus of tranquillity."

Maitreya asked, "Should the images on which one concentrates in observation be said to be different from the mind or not different?"

The Buddha answered, "They should be said to be no different, because those images are only consciousness. I say that the objects of consciousness are only manifestations of consciousness."

Maitreya asked, "If the images on which one concentrates are none other than the mind, how does the mind see the mind?"

The Buddha replied, "Herein there is nothing at all seeing anything at all. When this mind is aroused in this way, then there are such images appearing. It is like seeing something by means of a clean mirror with the object before it, thinking one is seeing an image, and thinking there is a separate image apart from the object. In the same way, when this mind is aroused, it seems as if different images focused on in concentration are appearing."

Maitreya asked, "If people naturally dwell on mental images such as form, are these too no different from mind?"

The Buddha answered, "They are also no different; but because of faulty awareness of these images, ignorant people do not realize they are only consciousness, and so they misunderstand them."

Maitreya inquired, "What is to be called sole practice of observation?"

The Buddha said, "If one continually focuses attention on meditation on mental appearances."

Maitreya asked, "What is to be called sole practice of tranquillity?"

The Buddha answered, "If one continually focuses attention on meditation on the uninterrupted mind."

Maitreya asked, "What is to be called combined operation of tranquillity and observation?"

The Buddha replied, "If one correctly meditates on one-pointedness of mind."

Maitreya inquired, "What are mental appearances?"

The Buddha said, "This means the images with discrimination that are objects of concentration in observation."

Maitreya asked, "What is the uninterrupted mind?"

The Buddha answered, "It is the mind that focuses on those images, itself the focus of tranquillity."

Maitreya asked, "What is one-pointedness of mind?"

The Buddha replied, "It means realizing that images concentrated on are only consciousness; or, realizing this, to meditate on suchness."

Maitreya inquired further of the Buddha, "How many kinds of observation are there?"

The Buddha answered, "In general, there are three: observation of appearances, investigative observation, and contemplative observation.

"Observation of appearances means observation purely meditating on the images with discrimination on which concentration is focused.

"Investigative observation means observation attentively meditating by means of intelligence in order to fully understand all that is not yet understood.

"Contemplative observation means observation attentively meditating by means of intelligence to truly realize all that is understood and to attain ultimate liberation."

Maitreya also asked the Buddha, "How many kinds of tranquillity are there?"

The Buddha replied, "There are also three, corresponding to the uninterrupted mind in the observation.

"Then again, there are also eight, one in each stage from the first meditation up to the state of neither perception nor nonperception.

"There is one kind of tranquillity, and there are also four, because there is one kind of tranquillity in each of the four immeasurables: immeasurable kindness, compassion, joy, and equanimity."

Maitreya also asked, "You say that there are tranquillity and observation that are in accord with the teaching, and there are tranquillity and observation that are not in accord with the Teaching. To what do these expressions refer?"

The Buddha said, "If enlightening beings attain tranquillity and observation in terms of the meaning of the teachings they have previously received and pondered, that is called tranquillity and observation in accord with the Teaching.

"If enlightening beings do not await teachings to be received and pondered, but just rely on the instructions of others and attain tranquillity and observation in terms of their meanings—such as, for example, contemplating decay and putrefaction, or the inconstancy of all conditioned things, or the painfulness of all conditioned things, or the selflessness of all phenomena, or nirvana as ultimate quiescence—such tranquillity and observation is said to be not in accord with the Teaching.

"Because they attain tranquillity and observation based on the Teaching, I define enlightening beings who practice in accord with the Teaching as being of keen faculties. Because they do not attain tranquillity and observation in accord with the Teaching, I define enlightening beings who practice according to faith as being of dull faculties."

Maitreya also asked the Buddha, "You speak of tranquillity and observation focused on different principles, and tranquillity and observation focused on all principles as a whole. What is the meaning of this?"

The Buddha said, "If enlightening beings focus on the principles of particular scriptures and cultivate tranquillity and observation based on the teachings they receive and contemplate, this is called tranquillity and observation focused on different principles.

"If they focus on the principles of all the scriptures, gather them into one whole, and attentively contemplate all these principles, approaching true suchness, directed toward true suchness, entering into true suchness, approaching enlightenment, approaching nirvana, approaching transformation of the mental basis, aiming for these and entering into these, reflecting that all these principles bespeak countless good practices, in this way cultivating tranquillity and observation, this is called tranquillity and observation focused on all principles as a whole."

Maitreya inquired, "The Buddha speaks of holistic tranquillity and observation with a small focus, with a great focus, and with an infinite focus. To what do these terms refer?"

The Buddha said, "If enlightening beings focus their attention on the doctrines of a particular scripture or treatise as one whole and meditate on them equally, that is holistic tranquillity and observation with a small focus.

"If they focus their attention on the principles of the scriptures they have received to contemplate as one whole and meditate on them equally, not focusing on them separately, this is tranquillity and observation with a great focus.

"If they focus their attention on the infinite teachings of the Buddha, the infinite statements of truth, the infinite awareness of ultimate wisdom, making them into one whole and meditating on them equally, not just on what they have received and think about, this is called tranquillity and observation with infinite focus."

Maitreya inquired, "What is attainment of tranquillity and observation focused on the totality of the teachings?"

The Buddha replied, "It is called attainment on five conditions.

"First is that the basis of all crude attachments is melted down from moment to moment in meditation.

"Second is that one becomes detached from miscellaneous thoughts and gets pleasure from spiritual enjoyment.

"Third is that one understands the measureless spiritual light of universal nondifferentiation.

"Fourth is that pure discrimination and nondiscrimination appropriate to fulfillment of what is to be done are constantly present.

"Fifth is that one embraces the bases of higher refinement in order to fulfill the spiritual body."

Maitreya asked, "In this tranquillity and observation focused on the totality of the teachings, what is called comprehension, and what is called attainment?"

The Buddha answered, "From the first stage of intense joy onward is called comprehension. From the third stage of radiance onward is called attainment.

"Enlightening beings in the beginning of practice also pursue this in their studies and concentrate on it. Although they are not yet worthy of praise, still they should not slacken or give up."

Maitreya went on to inquire, "This is tranquillity and observation. What is concentration with consideration and examination? What is concentration without consideration, only examination? What is concentration without consideration or examination?"

The Buddha replied, "If there is tranquillity and observation with grossly manifest reception and contemplation of the characteristics of the principles or phenomena one has taken up for consideration and examination, this is called concentration with consideration and examination.

"If there are no grossly manifest reception and contemplation of those characteristics, yet there are subtle mental reception and contemplation, this tranquillity and observation is called tranquillity and observation without consideration, only with examination.

"If there is no conscious reception or contemplation of the characteristics of any principles or phenomena at all, this tranquillity and observation is called concentration without consideration or examination.

"Also, searching tranquillity and observation is called concentration with consideration and examination. Investigative tranquillity and observation is called concentration with only examination and no consideration. Tranquillity and observation focused on the totality of reality is called concentration without consideration or examination."

Maitreya inquired, "What are stopping, arousal, and relinquishment?"

The Buddha replied, "If the mind is excited, or afraid of excitement, then concentration on undesirable things, or on the uninterrupted mind, is called stopping.

"If the mind is torpid, or afraid of torpor, then concentration on desirable things, or on the characteristics of the mind, is called arousal.

"When one practices only tranquillity or only observation, or is affected by afflictions when practicing both, effortless concentration and concentration in the spontaneous operation of mind is called relinquishment."

Maitreya also inquired, "You say enlightening beings practicing tranquillity and observation know doctrines and know meanings. What is knowing doctrines, what is knowing meaning?"

The Buddha said, "Enlightening beings know doctrines in five respects. They know their terms, statements, sounds, separateness, and totality.

"What are the terms? These refer to the temporary definitions of identifying concepts set up in reference to all pure and impure phenomena.

"What are statements? These are arrangements of words to explain the basis and establishment of the meanings of impurity and purity.

"What are the sounds? They are the utterances upon which the preceding two are based.

"What is knowing them separately? This means thought based on separate objects.

"What is knowing them in totality? This means thought based on the totality as object. In this way all are summed up into one, under the rubric of knowing doctrines.

"This is called an enlightening being's knowledge of doctrines. As for meanings, enlightening beings know them in ten respects. First, they know the nature of limits. Second, they know the nature of suchness. Third, they know the meaning of the experiencer. Fourth, they know the meaning of the experienced. Fifth, they know the meaning of structure. Sixth, they know the meaning of sustenance. Seventh, they know the meaning of error. Eighth, they know the meaning of absence of error. Ninth, they know the meaning of defilement. Tenth, they know the meaning of purity.

"The nature of limits refers to the bounds distinguishing the types of all defiled and pure phenomena.

"The nature of suchness means the true suchness in all defiled and pure phenomena. Of this there are seven types.

"First is the suchness of the mundane whirl; this refers to the beginninglessness and endlessness of all events.

"Second is the suchness of characteristics; this refers to the identitylessness and selflessness of all phenomena.

"Third is the suchness of discernment, which means that all events are essentially consciousness.

"Fourth is the suchness of setups, which is the holy truth of suffering that I explain.

"Fifth is the suchness of wrong action, which is the holy truth of causes of suffering that I explain.

"Sixth is the suchness of purity, which is the holy truth of extinction that I explain.

"Seventh is the suchness of right action, which is the holy truth of the path that I explain.

"In terms of the suchness of the mundane whirl, suchness of setups, and suchness of wrong action, all sentient beings are equal.

"In terms of the suchness of characteristics and the suchness of discernment, all things are equal.

"In terms of the suchness of purity, the enlightenment of saints, the enlightenment of individual illuminates, and supreme perfect enlightenment are equal.

"In terms of the suchness of right action, the wisdom in listening to the truth, focusing on the totality, and mastering tranquillity and observation are equal.

"The meaning of the experiencer refers to the five physical sense organs, mind, intellect, consciousness, and the various mental phenomena. The meaning of the experienced refers to the data of sense. Also, the experiencer is an object of perception too.

"The meaning of structure refers to the material world and all the realms of living beings therein. That is to say, one community, or a hundred communities, or a thousand communities, or a hundred thousand communities; or one land mass, or a hundred, a thousand, a hundred thousand land masses; or one continent, or a hundred, a thousand, a hundred thousand continents; or one world, or a hundred, a thousand, a hundred thousand worlds; or one solar system, or a hundred, a thousand, a hundred thousand solar systems; or one galaxy, or a hundred, a thousand, a hundred thousand galaxies; or one universe, or a hundred, a thousand, a hundred thousand, a million, a hundred million, a billion, a hundred billion, or countless universes, or the countless hundreds of thousands of atoms in a universe—all the innumerable material worlds in the ten directions.

"The meaning of sustenance refers to the necessities of life, the means of subsistence used by the various types of living beings.

"The meaning of error refers to errors of mind and view in reference to such things as the experiencer, thinking the impermanent to be permanent, thinking the painful to be pleasant, thinking the impure to be pure, thinking the selfless to be self. The meaning of absence of error is the opposite of this, and is a cure for this.

"The meaning of defilement refers to three kinds of defilement in the triple world: the defilement of afflictions, the defilement of actions, and the defilement of birth.

"The meaning of purity refers to the elements of enlightenment detached from these three kinds of defilement.

"You should know that these ten types contain all meanings."

The Buddha also said, "Enlightening beings are said to know meaning because of knowing five kinds of meaning. What five meanings? First is completely knowing phenomena. Second is completely knowing significations. Third is completely knowing causes. Fourth is completely knowing effects. Fifth is awakened comprehension of this.

"Here, completely knowing phenomena refers to all that is

known, such as the clusters of material and mental elements, the sense organs, the sense data, and so on.

"Knowing significations refers to the spheres of all the different categories and distinctions there are to be known: mundane convention, ultimate truth, virtues, faults, conditions, time frames, origination, subsistence, disintegration, things like sickness, suffering and its causes, true suchness, reality, the cosmos, details and generalities, all-embracing answers, particularized answers, answering after returning a question, answering by not answering, the hidden and the revealed, and so on.

"Completely knowing causes refers to the means by which enlightenment is attained, such as the points of mindfulness and the right efforts.

"Completely knowing effects refers to the discipline in which greed, hatred, and stupidity are forever ended, the results of asceticism by which greed, hatred, and stupidity are forever ended, and the realization of the worldly and transcendental virtues of Buddhas and their disciples.

"Awakened comprehension of this refers to teaching others the liberations and knowledges in the aforementioned realizations.

"These five meanings include all meanings.

"Also, enlightening beings are said to know meaning by virtue of knowing four kinds of meaning: the meaning of mental grasping, the meaning of reception, the meaning of discernment, and the meaning of defilement and purity. These four meanings embrace all meanings.

"Also enlightening beings are said to know meaning by virtue of knowing three kinds of meanings: the meaning of statements, the meaning of meanings, and the meaning of realms.

"The meaning of statements refers to bodies of words.

"The meaning of meanings is of ten kinds: reality, complete knowledge, annihilation, realization, cultivation, distinctions of the foregoing, interdependence of object and subject, barriers to complete knowledge, elements conducive to knowledge, and the faults and merits of nescience and knowledge.

"The meaning of realms refers to five realms: the material world, the realm of sentient beings, the realm of truth, the realm of pacification, and the realm of means of pacification.

"These three meanings embrace all meanings."

Maitreya also inquired, "What are the differences among knowing meaning by wisdom realized by learning, by wisdom realized by thinking, and by wisdom realized by practice of tranquillity and observation?"

The Buddha replied, "Wisdom consisting of learning is based on words and only conforms to explanation; one still has not skillfully directed the mind or actualized the Teaching. One follows liberation but cannot yet take in the meaning of attainment of liberation.

"Wisdom produced by thinking is also based on words, but it is not merely literal; one also skillfully directs the mind. But one does not yet actualize the Teaching. One follows liberation even more but still cannot yet take in the meaning of attainment of liberation.

"As for enlightening beings' wisdom realized by practice, it is both based on words and not based on words, both according to the explanation and not according to the explanation; they skillfully direct their minds to what is to be known, and the corresponding images on which concentration is focused actually appear. They ultimately conform to liberation and are able to take in the meaning of attainment of liberation. This is called the distinction of the three kinds of knowing."

Maitreya also asked, "As enlightening beings who cultivate tranquillity and observation know doctrines and meanings, what is knowledge, what is vision?"

The Buddha replied, "I explain the distinction between

knowledge and vision in countless ways, but now I will tell you about their characteristics in a general way. If one cultivates tranquillity and observation focused on the totality of the teachings, the subtle wisdom therein is called knowledge. If one cultivates tranquillity and observation focused on particular teachings, the subtle wisdom therein is called vision."

Maitreya also asked, "When enlightening beings practice tranquillity and observation, on what do they focus attention? Of what, and how, do they dismiss appearances?"

The Buddha answered, "By putting their attention on true suchness, they dismiss the appearances of phenomena and the appearances of significations. When one does not apprehend names or nominality, and does not look at the appearances on which they are based, they are thus dismissed.

"As with names, the same applies to phrases and statements and all significations; and finally, when one does not apprehend any realms or their natures, and also does not look at the appearances on which they are based, they are thus dismissed."

Maitreya asked, "What about the appearances of true suchness realized; are the appearances of true suchness also to be dismissed?"

The Buddha answered, "In the true suchness that enlightening beings realize, there are no appearances, and there is nothing apprehended at all; what could be dismissed? I say that when one knows suchness, that overcomes the signifying appearances of all things, while this realization cannot be overcome by anything else."

Maitreya said, "You explain, by way of metaphor, that just as one cannot see one's own face in a vessel of turbid water, in a dirty mirror, or in an agitated pond, one cannot observe suchness accurately if one does not cultivate the mind properly. What is the observing mind to which reference is made here, and upon what suchness is this explanation based?"

The Buddha answered, "This refers to three kinds of observing mind: the observing mind developed by learning, the observing mind developed by thinking, and the observing mind developed by practice. This explanation is based on the suchness of perception."

Maitreya asked, "When enlightening beings who know the meaning of the Teaching in this way cultivate practice to dismiss appearances, what kinds of appearances are hard to dismiss, and who can dismiss them?"

The Buddha replied, "There are ten kinds of such appearances, and emptiness can dismiss them.

"First, there is the appearance of various words, because of knowing doctrines. This can be properly dismissed by the emptiness of all things.

"Second, there is the appearance of birth and death, subsistence and change, and the appearance of continuous succession, because of knowing the suchness of setups. These can be properly dismissed by the emptiness of appearances and the emptiness of nonsuccession.

"Third, there is the appearance of attachment to the body, and the appearance of conceit, because of knowing the experiencer. These can be properly dismissed by the emptiness of the internal and the emptiness of ungraspability.

"Fourth, there is the appearance of attachment to provisions, because of knowing the experienced. This can be properly dismissed by the emptiness of the external.

"Fifth, there is the internal appearance of comfort, and the external appearance of charm, because of knowing about sustenance, corresponding to goods and services. These can be properly dismissed by internal and external emptiness and the emptiness of inherent nature.

"Sixth, there is the appearance of infinity, because of knowing structures. This is properly dismissed by the emptiness of magnitude.

"Seventh, there is the appearance of inner quiescence and liberation, because of knowing formlessness. This is properly dismissed by the emptiness of the created.

"Eighth, there is the appearance of selflessness of persons and selflessness of phenomena, or the appearance of consciousness only and the appearance of ultimate truth, because of knowing the meaning of true suchness of characteristics. These are properly dismissed by ultimate emptiness, the emptiness of essencelessness, the emptiness of inherent nature, and the emptiness of ultimate truth.

"Ninth, there are the appearances of the uncreated and of changelessness, because of knowing the meaning of pure suchness. These are properly dismissed by the emptiness of the uncreate and the emptiness of changelessness.

"Tenth, there is the appearance of emptiness, because of conscious thought of those curative emptinesses. This is properly dismissed by the emptiness of emptiness."

Maitreya asked, "When one gets rid of these ten kinds of appearances, then what appearances does one get rid of, and from what appearances is one liberated?"

The Buddha replied, "One gets rid of the appearances of the images focused on in concentration, and one attains liberation from the appearances of defilement and bondage; and this too is dismissed.

"You should realize that, speaking in terms of predominance, to say that such and such an emptiness quells such and such an appearance does not mean that each emptiness cannot quell all appearances. It is like the fact that ignorance produces all defiled elements of existence, all the way up to old age and death, but speaking in terms of predominance we just say that ignorance produces actions, because these actions are the most immediate relation."

Maitreya then asked the Buddha, "Herein, what is the nature of total emptiness, such that if enlightening beings know this they will not miss the nature of emptiness and will be free of presumptuous conceit?"

The Buddha replied, "Very good! It is good that you ask the Buddha about the profound meaning of this, so that enlightening beings will not miss the nature of emptiness. Why? Because if enlightening beings miss the nature of emptiness, they miss the whole great vehicle. So listen well and I will explain.

"All kinds of conceptual images, defiled or pure, imposed on the relative and real aspects of phenomena are ultimately unconnected, and nothing can be grasped therein. This is called the nature of total emptiness in the great vehicle."

Maitreya asked, "How many kinds of higher concentration can this tranquillity and observation include?"

The Buddha said, "As I say, innumerable hearers, enlightening beings, and Buddhas have innumerable higher concentrations; know that all of them are included in this."

Maitreya asked, "What is the causal basis of this tranquillity and observation?"

The Buddha replied, "Pure conduct and right insight produced by pure learning and thinking."

Maitreya asked, "What is the result?"

The Buddha replied, "A pure mind and pure intellect. Also, all of the worldly and supramundane virtues of all hearers and Buddhas are results of this tranquillity and observation."

Maitreya inquired, "What work can this tranquillity and observation perform?"

The Buddha answered, "It can free one from two kinds of bondage: bondage by appearances, and bondage by afflictions."

Maitreya asked, "The Buddha says that there are five kinds

of entanglement. Among them, how many are hindrances to tranquillity, how many are hindrances to observation, and how many are hindrances to both?"

The Buddha replied, "Attachment to the body and possessions is a hindrance to tranquillity. Inability to follow and aspire to the enlightening teachings is a hindrance to observation. Fondness for miscellaneous company and being satisfied with a little are hindrances to both: one cannot perform practice because of the first, and practice cannot reach the ultimate end because of the second."

Maitreya asked, "Among the five veils, how many are hindrances to tranquillity, how many are hindrances to observation, and how many are hindrances to both?"

The Buddha answered, "Agitation and wrong action hinder tranquillity. Oblivion, sleepiness, and doubt hinder observation. Craving and resentment hinder both."

Maitreya asked, "What can be called attainment of complete purity of the path of tranquillity?"

The Buddha answered, "When all oblivion and sleepiness are properly removed, that is called attainment of complete purity of the path of tranquillity."

Maitreya asked, "What can be called attainment of complete purity of the path of observation?"

The Buddha answered, "When all agitation and wrong action are properly removed, that is called attainment of complete purity of the path of observation."

Maitreya inquired, "When tranquillity and observation are actualized, how many kinds of mental distractions should enlightening beings know about?"

The Buddha answered, "They should know about five kinds of distraction. First is distraction of thought. Second is external distraction. Third is internal distraction. Fourth is distraction by appearances. Fifth is distraction by grossness.

"If enlightening beings give up thoughts appropriate to the Great Vehicle, and fall into thoughts appropriate to hearers and individual illuminates, this is called distraction of thought.

"Vexations accompanying thoughts pursuing the motley appearances of external objects of desire, and the scattering of the mind indulging in external objects, are called external distraction.

"The defilement of subsidiary afflictions due to torpor, drowsiness, or oblivion, or attachment to concentration, or following one concentration, is called internal distraction.

"If, depending on external appearances, one thinks about the appearances on which internal concentration plays, this is called distraction by appearances.

"If one produces feelings in connection with internal thought, and conceives of self based on the gross body, and produces conceit, that is called distraction by grossness."

Maitreya inquired, "What barriers can this tranquillity and observation overcome, from the first stage of enlightening to the stage of realization of enlightenment?"

The Buddha answered, "In the first stage, this tranquillity and observation overcome the barrier of defilements produced by the active expression of afflictions of bad tendencies.

"In the second stage, they overcome the barrier of active expression of subtle errors.

"In the third stage, they overcome the barrier of desire.

"In the fourth stage, they overcome the barrier of attachment to concentration states, and the barrier of attachment to religion.

"In the fifth stage, they overcome the barrier of total rejection and pursuit in regard to the birth-death cycle and nirvana.

"In the sixth stage, they overcome the barrier of multifarious mental patterns.

"In the seventh stage, they overcome the barrier of subtle mental patterns.

"In the eighth stage, they overcome the barrier of effort in regard to the formless, and the barrier of lack of freedom in regard to that which has form.

"In the ninth stage, they overcome the barrier of lack of mastery of all kinds of verbal expressions used as teaching devices.

"In the tenth stage, they overcome the barrier of not attaining full realization of the spiritual body.

"In the stage of realization of enlightenment, this tranquillity and observation overcome the barrier of the extremely subtle and most extremely subtle afflictions, as well as the barrier of knowledge.

"Because they are able to permanently destroy such barriers, one ultimately attains unattached, unobstructed total knowledge and vision. The supremely pure spiritual body is defined in reference to the fulfillment of what is to be done."

Maitreya also asked the Buddha, "How do enlightening beings cultivate practice based on tranquillity and observation so as to realize supreme perfect enlightenment?"

The Buddha said, "If enlightening beings, having attained tranquillity and observation, based on the seven kinds of true suchness, inwardly contemplate suchness correctly by a mind supremely concentrated on the truths they learn and consider, in terms of proper ascertainment and proper thought, on the proper basis, because they correctly contemplate true suchness they can get rid of all subtle mental patterns, to say nothing of coarse ones.

"These subtle appearances refer to what the minds grasps: sensations, perceptions, discriminations, notions of defilement and purity, notions of internal and external, notions that they should strive to benefit all sentient beings, notions of right knowledge, notions of suchness, notions of suffering, its cause, its extinction, and the way, notions of the created and the uncreated, notions of permanence and impermanence, notions of the nature of suffering as changing or changeless, notions of variety or uniformity of the created, the notions of all things inherent in knowing everything, or notions of the selflessness of persons or the selflessness of things.

"Enlightening beings can get rid of all these mental patterns. Having persisted much in such practice, they skillfully cure the mind of all those entanglements, veils, and distractions.

"After this, there are seven individual inner realizations in respect to the seven kinds of true suchness, the knowledge born of which is called the path of insight.

"By virtue of attainment of this, they are said to enter the true nature of enlightening beings, to be free from rebirth, to be born in the family of Buddhas, and to realize the first stage. They are also able to experience the excellent qualities of this stage.

"By virtue of having previously attained tranquillity and observation, they will have already attained two kinds of perceptions: perception of images with discrimination, and perception of images without discrimination. Now, by virtue of attainment of the path of insight, they also realize perception of the bounds of phenomena, and go on in subsequent stages to progressively practice the path of cultivation, and so meditate attentively on these three perceptions.

"Just as a man may use a slender wedge to remove a stout wedge, so does an enlightening being, using this method of extracting a wedge with a wedge, get rid of internal patterns, so that all patterns involved in defilement are removed. Because these patterns are removed, grossness is also removed; and because of permanently destroying all notional patterns, then the mind is gradually refined in subsequent stages, even as gold is refined, until finally one realizes the mind of supreme perfect enlightenment by correct practice of internal tranquillity and observation."

Maitreya also inquired, "How does one cultivate practice so as to draw forth the immense power of enlightening beings?"

The Buddha replied, "If enlightening beings thoroughly know six points, then they can draw forth the immense power proper to enlightening beings. First is knowing the arising of the mind. Second is knowing the abiding of the mind. Third is knowing the emancipation of the mind. Fourth is knowing the increase of the mind. Fifth is knowing the decrease of the mind. Sixth is knowing expedient methods.

"What is knowing the arising of the mind? It means accurately knowing the differentiations of sixteen patterns of mental arising.

"The first is the arising of the perduring consciousness of matter, which itself cannot be consciously known; this is called the clinging consciousness.

"The second is the arising of consciousness focused on various transient appearances. This means the discriminating cognitive consciousness that grasps all objects, such as forms, as well as the awareness that grasps inner and outer objects, or the cognitive consciousness that suddenly enters many concentrations, see many Buddha-lands and sees many Buddhas.

"Third is the arising of consciousness focused on the small. This refers to consciousness hooked onto the realm of desire.

"Fourth is the arising of consciousness focused on the large. This refers to consciousness hooked onto the realm of form.

"Fifth is the arising of consciousness focused on the measureless. This refers to consciousness hooked onto the infinity of space, or the infinity of consciousness.

"Sixth is the arising of consciousness focused on the infinitesimal. This refers to consciousness hooked onto nothingness.

"Seventh is the arising of consciousness focused on limitation. This refers to consciousness hooked onto the state of neither perception nor nonperception.

"Eighth is the arising of formless consciousness. This refers to transmundane consciousness and consciousness focused on extinction.

"Ninth is the arising of consciousness operating with suffering. This refers to the consciousness of hells.

"Tenth is the arising of consciousness operating with mixed feelings. This refers to consciousness with active desires.

"Eleventh is the arising of consciousness operating with joy. This refers to consciousness in the first two stages of meditation.

"Twelfth is the arising of consciousness operating with bliss. This refers to consciousness in the third stage of meditation.

"Thirteenth is the arising of consciousness with neither pain nor pleasure. This refers to consciousness from the fourth stage of meditation up to the state of neither perception nor nonperception.

"Fourteenth is the arising of consciousness with defilement. This refers to consciousness connected with afflictions.

"Fifteenth is the arising of consciousness with virtue. This refers to consciousness connected with faith and so on.

"Sixteenth is the arising of neutral consciousness. This refers to consciousness not connected with either defilement or virtue.

"What is knowing the abiding of the mind? It means truly knowing the suchness of perception.

"What is knowing the emancipation of the mind? It means truly knowing emancipation from two kinds of bondage: bondage by appearances and bondage by grossness.

"What is knowing the increase of the mind? It means truly knowing that the mind which can quell bondage by appearances and grossness can increase when they increase.

"What is knowing the decrease of the mind? It means truly

knowing that the mind defiled by appearances and grossness decreases as they decrease when quelled.

"What is knowing expedient methods? It means truly knowing the liberations, the points of dominance, and the points of totality, for cultivation or purification.

"This is how enlightening beings have brought, do bring, and will bring forth the immense power of enlightening beings."

Maitreya also asked the Buddha, "You say that in the realm of nirvana without remaining dependency, all sensations eternally cease. What sensations eternally cease?"

The Buddha answered, "Essentially there are two kinds of sensations that eternally cease. One is sensation of subjective grossness. Second is sensation of objects resulting therefrom.

"There are four kinds of sensation of subjective grossness. First is sensation of the material part of the person. Second is sensation of the immaterial part of the person. Third is sensation of grossness of effects already developed, meaning sensation of the present. Fourth is sensation of effects as yet undeveloped, meaning sensation of future causes.

"There are also four kinds of sensation of resulting objects. One is sensation of the basis of support. Second is sensation of means of subsistence. Third is sensation of use. Fourth is sensation of attachment.

"In the realm of nirvana without remaining dependency, sensations of effects as yet undeveloped are all extinct, while the sensation of the curative feeling of clarity is present in all cases. In some cases, the sensations of effects already developed, or both of the two aforementioned kinds of sensation, are all extinct, and there is only the present sensation of the feeling of clarity. In the realm of nirvana without remaining dependency, at the time of ultimate parinirvana, this also passes away forever. This is why it is said that in the realm of nirvana without remaining dependency, all sensations cease eternally, without remainder."

Then, having said all this to Maitreya, the Buddha went on to say, "It is very good how you have managed to question the Buddha based on the fully complete, most utterly pure path of mystic yoga. You have attained definite, ultimate skill in yoga. I have explained to you the fully complete, most utterly pure path of mystic yoga, which has been and will be explained by all Buddhas of the past and future. Good men and women should all work diligently on this and practice correctly."

Then, in order to recapitulate, the Buddha said in verse:

In the yoga provisionally set up in the Teaching,
If one is negligent, one will lose a great benefit.
If one practices correctly based on this Teaching and yoga,
One will attain great awakening.
If one sees there is something to gain, one cannot escape;
If one says this view is attainment of the Teaching,
Maitreya, one is as far from yoga
As the earth is from the sky.
Helping people steadfastly without artifice,
Having awakened, striving for the benefit of the living:
The wise do this throughout the ages,
And so attain the supreme joy of nondefilement.
If people preach because of desire,
They are said to have given up desire only to grasp
    desire again.
Ignoramuses who get the priceless jewel of the Teaching
Turn right around and go on wandering, begging,
Clinging to argumentation and nonsense;
They should give it up and exert higher efforts.
In order to liberate people,
You learn this yoga.

Then Maitreya asked the Buddha, "World Honored One, within this teaching of unlocking mysteries, what should this teaching be called, and how should it be preserved?"

The Buddha replied, "This is called the definitive teaching of yoga. You should maintain this definitive teaching of yoga."

When the Buddha explained this definitive teaching of yoga, six hundred thousand people in the audience were inspired with the determination for complete perfect enlightenment. Three hundred thousand disciples became detached from sense data and freed from defilement, and attained purity of objective insight into things. One hundred and fifty thousand disciples ended all contamination forever, and their minds became liberated. Seventy-five thousand enlightening beings attained great yogic meditation.

7. THE TRANSCENDENT WAYS OF THE STAGES

Then the enlightening being Avalokiteshvara said to the Buddha, "The Buddha speaks of ten stages of enlightening beings: the stage of intense joy, the stage of freedom from defilement, the stage of radiance, the stage of blazing intellect, the stage most difficult to conquer, the stage of presence, the stage of far going, the stage of immovability, the stage of good intellect, and the stage of cloud of teaching. You also speak of Buddhahood, making eleven stages. How many kinds of purity, in how many portions, are these stages contained in?"

The Buddha said, "The stages are contained by four kinds of purity in eleven portions. What does it mean to say that four kinds of purity can contain the stages? Purity of overwhelming determination contains the first stage, purity of overwhelming discipline contains the second stage, purity of overwhelming concentration contains the third stage, and purity of overwhelming insight become more and more refined in successive stages, so it includes the stages from the fourth stage up to Buddhahood.

"What does it mean to say that eleven portions contain the stages? First, in the stage of devoted practice, enlightening beings cultivate the tolerance of devotion extremely well, and therefore go beyond that stage and experientially enter the true nature of enlightening beings, detached from life. Due to these cooperating factors, this portion is complete in these enlightening beings, yet they still cannot act with correct knowledge of active expressions of subtle errors and faults.

"In order to fulfill this portion, they diligently practice so that they can realize it. Due to these cooperating factors, this portion is fulfilled, but they are still not able to attain the full potential of meditation and concentration in the world, or the mental control to remember what they hear and learn.

"Therefore they are still incomplete in this portion, and in order to fulfill this portion they practice diligently so as to be able to attain it. As a result, this portion is completed, but they are not yet able to command the elements of enlightenment they have attained and practiced and concentrated on so much, and they are unable to give up their attachments to concentration states and religious practices. Therefore they are still incomplete in this respect.

"In order to fulfill this next portion, they practice diligently so as to actually realize it. Therefore they become complete in this respect, but are still unable to truly observe the principles of the truths, and are unable to abandon one-sided attraction or aversion for life and death and nirvana. They are also unable to practice the elements of enlightenment included in expedients. Because of this, they are still incomplete in this respect, and they practice diligently to realize this portion and so fulfill it.

"Because of this, they complete this portion, but they are as yet unable to truly see through the continuing cycles of becoming and decay; and because they develop much revulsion to becoming and decay, they are unable to dwell much on formless attention. Therefore they are still incomplete in this respect, and practice diligently to realize this portion and fulfill it. As a result, they become complete in this respect, but they still cannot make formless attention flawless and uninterrupted and highly cultivated. Therefore they are still incomplete in this respect.

"In order to fulfill this portion, they practice diligently to realize it. Due to this, they become complete in this respect, but they are as yet unable to relinquish effort in the formless state, and they are as yet unable to master forms. Therefore they are still incomplete in this respect.

"In order to fulfill this portion, they practice diligently to realize it. Due to this, they become complete in this respect, but they are as yet unable to attain great freedom in teaching with different terms, different forms, and different expressions, to all kinds of people. Therefore they are still incomplete in this respect.

"In order to fulfill this portion, they practice diligently to realize it. Due to this, they become complete in this respect, but they still do not attain direct experience of the perfect spiritual body. Therefore they are still incomplete in this respect.

"In order to fulfill this portion, they practice diligently to realize it. Due to this, they become complete in this respect, yet they are still incapable of unattached, unobstructed subtle knowledge and subtle vision of all objects of knowledge. Therefore they are still incomplete in this respect.

"In order to fulfill this portion, they practice diligently to realize it. Due to this, they become complete in this respect, and therefore all the portions are fulfilled. These eleven portions contain all the stages."

Avalokiteshvara also asked the Buddha, "Why is the first stage called the stage of extreme joy? And why are the other stages, up to the stage of Buddhahood, called what they are?"

The Buddha replied, "Accomplishing a great aim, attaining a world-transcending mind for the first time, one becomes very joyful. The first stage is therefore called that of intense joy.

"By virtue of avoiding all transgressions, even minute ones, the second stage is called the stage of freedom from defilement, or purity.

"The third stage is called the stage of radiance because the concentration and mental control attained in this stage are a basis for immeasurable light of knowledge.

"The fourth stage is called the stage of blazing intellect because the elements of enlightenment one attains in this stage burn out afflictions with knowledge like flames of fire.

"The fifth stage is called the stage difficult to conquer because one attains mastery only after extreme difficulty in practicing the techniques of the elements of enlightenment.

"The sixth stage is called the stage of presence because one observes the flux of events at the moment, and because after a great deal of meditation upon the formless, it becomes manifest.

"The seventh stage is called the stage of far going because one in this stage realizes flawless, uninterrupted formless attention to a great extent, and is on the brink of purity.

"The eighth stage is called the stage of immovability by virtue of attainment of effortlessness in dealing with the formless, and not being moved by currently active afflictions in the midst of forms.

"The ninth stage is called the stage of good intellect because of mastery of all kinds of spiritual teaching and attainment of tremendous unimpeded knowing.

"The tenth stage is called cloud of teaching because the gross body is as vast as space and the spiritual body is fulfilled, like a great cloud that can cover all.

"The eleventh stage is called the stage of Buddhahood because of permanently stopping the most subtle barriers of afflictions and knowledge, being unattached and unobstructed in dealing with all kinds of objects of knowledge, and realizing true enlightenment."

Avalokiteshvara also asked the Buddha, "How many kinds of ignorance and grossness are there to be cured in these stages?"

The Buddha replied, "There are twenty-two kinds of ignorance and eleven kinds of grossness to be cured in these stages.

"In the first stage, there are two kinds of ignorance. One is the ignorance of clinging to person and thing. The other is ignorance of the defilement of wrong tendencies and actions. These and their grossness are what is to be cured.

"In the second stage, there are two kinds of ignorance. One is ignorance of minute errors and transgressions. The other is ignorance of what various actions lead to. These and their grossness are what is to be cured.

"In the third stage, there are two kinds of ignorance. One is ignorance of greed. The other is ignorance of complete mental control to retain what is learned. These and their grossness are what is to be cured.

"In the fourth stage, there are two kinds of ignorance. One is ignorance of attachment to attainments in concentration. The other is ignorance of attachment to religion. These and their grossness are what is to be cured.

"In the fifth stage, there are two kinds of ignorance. One is ignorance of one-sided thought rejecting life and death. The other is ignorance of one-sided thought heading for nirvana. These and their grossness are what is to be cured.

"In the sixth stage, there are two kinds of ignorance. One is ignorance of observing the flux of events at the moment. The other is ignorance of elaborate active mental patterns. These and their grossness are what is to be cured.

"In the seventh stage, there are two kinds of ignorance. One is ignorance of subtle active mental patterns. The other is ignorance of method in one-sided formless awareness. These and their grossness are what is to be cured.

"In the eighth stage, there are two kinds of ignorance. One is ignorance of making effort toward the formless. The other is ignorance of control over forms. These and their grossness are what is to be cured.

"In the ninth stage, there are two kinds of ignorance. One

is ignorance of control of the intellectual powers and mental command of ultimate understanding of infinite expressions of truth. The other is ignorance of free command of special knowledge of comprehension and communication. These and their grossness are what is to be cured.

"In the tenth stage, there are two kinds of ignorance. One is ignorance of great mystic powers. The other is ignorance of awakening to subtle mysteries. These and their grossness are what is to be cured.

"In the stage of Buddhahood, coming to thusness, there are two kinds of ignorance. One is ignorance of extremely subtle sticking to objects of knowledge. The other is ignorance of extremely subtle barriers. These and their grossness are what is to be cured.

"The stages are set up because of these twenty-two kinds of ignorance and eleven kinds of grossness. Supreme perfect enlightenment is free from bondage to them."

The enlightening being Avalokiteshvara said to the Buddha, "Supreme perfect enlightenment is most marvelous and effects great benefits, great rewards, enabling enlightening beings to break through such great webs of ignorance and to get past such great wilds of grossness and to actually realize supreme perfect enlightenment in the present."

Avalokiteshvara then went on to ask the Buddha, "In these stages, how many kinds of excellence are defined?"

The Buddha replied, "In brief, there are eight. First is purity of strong determination. Second is purity of mind. Third is purity of compassion. Fourth is purity of transcendence. Fifth is purity of seeing Buddhas and offering service. Sixth is purity of maturing sentient beings. Seventh is purity of birth. Eighth is purity of spiritual powers.

"These purities in the first stage increase and improve from stage to stage, to the purities of Buddhahood, except that there is no purity of birth in the stage of Buddhahood.

"Also, the virtues in the first stage all exist equally in the higher stages, so you should know that the virtues of each stage are excellent, but the virtues of the ten stages of all enlightening beings all have something above them. The virtues of the stage of Buddhahood, in contrast, have nothing above them."

The enlightening being Avalokiteshvara also asked the Buddha, "Why do you say the birth of enlightening beings is most excellent among living beings?"

The Buddha replied, "There are four reasons. First, because it is constructed on ultimately pure foundations of good. Second, because it is chosen intentionally, with conscious discernment. Third, because it is based on compassion, to liberate sentient beings. Fourth, because one can be undefiled oneself and remove the defilements of others."

Avalokiteshvara also asked the Buddha, "Why do you say enlightening beings carry out far-reaching vows, marvelous vows, excellent vows?"

The Buddha replied, "For four reasons. Enlightening beings do know the bliss of nirvana very well and can quickly realize it, yet they relinquish immediate experience of the state of bliss and arouse a mind of great aspiration to benefit living beings, without object, without expectation, and therefore they remain in the midst of many kinds of suffering over a long time. That is why I say that enlightening beings carry out far-reaching, marvelous, excellent vows."

The enlightening being Avalokiteshvara also asked the Buddha, "How many things should enlightening beings learn?"

The Buddha replied, "In general, there are six things enlightening beings should learn: consummate giving, discipline, forbearance, diligence, meditation, and insight."

Avalokiteshvara asked, "Of these things to learn, how many

are included in the study of discipline, how many are included in the study of mental concentration, and how many are included in the study of knowledge?"

The Buddha replied, "The first three are included in the study of discipline. Meditation is included in the study of concentration. Insight is included in the study of knowledge. And I say diligence is in all of them."

Avalokiteshvara asked, "Of these six things to learn, how many are included in provisions of virtue, and how many are included in provisions of knowledge?"

The Buddha replied, "Whatever is included in the study of discipline is said to be included in provisions of virtue. Whatever is included in the study of knowledge is said to be included in provisions of knowledge. Diligence and meditation I say are in both provisions of virtue and knowledge."

Avalokiteshvara also asked, "How should enlightening beings cultivate these six things to learn?"

The Buddha replied, "They should cultivate them by five kinds of unification practice. First is intense devotion to the subtle correct teachings dealing with the ways of transcendence for enlightening beings. Second is diligent cultivation of subtle knowledge developed by learning, contemplating, and applying ten kinds of spiritual practice. Third is preserving the will for enlightenment in all situations. Fourth is associating with the wise. Fifth is constantly working to cultivate good."

Avalokiteshvara asked, "Why, as you define these things to learn, are there only six?"

The Buddha replied, "For two reasons. One is to benefit sentient beings. The other is to cure afflictions. The first three benefit sentient beings; the latter three cure all afflictions.

"As for the first three benefiting sentient beings, because of giving, enlightening beings use means of subsistence for the benefit of sentient beings, to help and aid them. Because of discipline, they do not act in harmful or oppressive or irritating ways, and thus they benefit sentient beings. Because of forbearance, they are able to bear injury, oppression, and annoyance by others, and thus benefit sentient beings.

"As for the latter three curing afflictions, because of diligence, although enlightening beings may not have yet subdued all afflictions forever or destroyed all propensities forever, still they diligently practice good, and those afflictions cannot upset their worthy efforts. By meditation, they permanently subdue afflictions. By insight, they permanently destroy propensities."

Avalokiteshvara asked, "Why, as you define the other ways of transcendence, are there only four more?"

The Buddha said, "Because they are aids to the first six ways of transcendence. Enlightening beings use skill in means of salvation to deal with sentient beings to be saved by the first three ways of transcendence, and place them in good. Therefore I say the transcendent way of skill in means is an aid to the first three ways of transcendence.

"If there are many afflictions in the present state, and so people are incapable of cultivation and continuity, and they have weak wills and inferior aspirations and so are incapable of inner mental stability, and are unable to hear the teachings for enlightening beings and cultivate good, therefore their meditations cannot bring forth transmundane wisdom; so they take in a little bit of narrow inferior virtue and truly vow in their hearts that in the future their afflictions will diminish. This is called the transcendent way of vowing. By this vowing, afflictions are weakened and diligence can be cultivated, so I say that the transcendent way of vowing is an aid to the transcendent way of diligence.

"If enlightening beings associate with good people, listen to true teaching, and think about it reasonably, and thereby transform inferior will into superior will, and can also attain higher aspiration, this is called the transcendent way of power. By this power, they have the capability of inner mental stability, so I say the transcendent way of power is an aid to the transcendent way of meditation.

"If enlightening beings are able to hear the teachings for enlightening beings, focus on what is good, and cultivate its practice, they can develop meditation. This is called the transcendent way of knowledge, by virtue of which knowledge they are able to bring out transmundane wisdom. Therefore I say that the transcendental way of knowledge is an aid to the transcendental way of insight."

Avalokiteshvara asked, "Why do you explain the six ways of transcendence in this order?"

The Buddha replied, "Because each is a basis for subsequent development. That is to say, if enlightening beings are not obsessed with themselves and their goods, then they can keep pure discipline. To keep pure discipline, they practice forbearance. Having cultivated forbearance, they can develop diligence. Having developed diligence, they can master meditation. With meditation, they can attain transmundane wisdom. That is why I explain the ways of transcendence in this order."

The enlightening being Avalokiteshvara also asked the Buddha, "How many different kinds of each of the six transcendent ways are there?"

The Buddha replied, "There are three kinds. The three kinds of giving are giving of teaching, giving of goods, and giving of fearlessness.

"The three kinds of discipline are the discipline of increasingly giving up what is not good, the discipline of increasingly developing what is good, and the discipline of increasingly benefiting sentient beings.

"The three kinds of forbearance are the forbearance of bearing injury, the forbearance of serenity in suffering, and the forbearance of truthful observation of realities.

"The three kinds of diligence are diligence as armor, diligence of concerted effort to increasingly develop good qualities, and diligence of concentrated effort to help sentient beings.

"The three kinds of meditation are meditation in a state of bliss without discriminating thought, still and silent, extremely tranquil and impeccable, thus curing the pains of afflictions; meditation that brings forth virtuous qualities and powers; and meditation that brings forth benefit for sentient beings.

"The three kinds of insight are insight focused on conventional worldly truth, insight focused on ultimate truth, and insight focused on benefiting sentient beings."

Avalokiteshvara also asked, "Why are the transcendent ways named transcendent ways?"

The Buddha replied, "For five reasons: no defiling habits; no attachment; no fault; no discrimination; proper dedication. No defiling habits means not sticking to anything inconsistent with the transcendent ways. No attachment means the mind is not tied to the ripening of the fruits and the rewards of the transcendent ways. No fault means that there are no defiling things mixed up in these transcendent ways and they are carried out skillfully without error. No discrimination means not clinging literally to the individual characteristics of the transcendent ways. Proper dedication means dedicating the transcendent ways one has performed and developed to the quest for supreme perfect enlightenment."

Avalokiteshvara asked, "What do you call things that are inconsistent with the transcendent ways?"

The Buddha replied, "In general, there are six kinds. First, seeing profound worth and advantage in all pleasures such as happiness, sensual enjoyment, wealth, and dominion. Second, seeing profound worth and advantage in the acts, words, and thoughts indulged in the pursuit of enjoyments. Third, seeing profound worth and advantage in not enduring the scorn of others. Fourth, seeing profound worth and advantage in not cultivating religious practices and in clinging to pleasures. Fifth, seeing profound worth and advantage in confused activities in the midst of the hustle and bustle of society. Sixth, seeing profound worth and advantage in what one perceives, feels, and cognizes, in talk and nonsense."

Avalokiteshvara asked the Buddha, "What are different fruits of all these ways of transcendence?"

The Buddha replied, "In brief, there are six: gaining great wealth; being reborn in a good condition; having no enemies, no disruption, and much joy and happiness; being a leader of people; having no physical disturbance or injury; having a great clan."

Avalokiteshvara asked the Buddha, "What are the things that adulterate the ways of transcendence?"

The Buddha replied, "This generally comes from four kinds of religious practice: practice without compassion, incorrect practice, inconsistent practice, or careless practice. Incorrect practice means straying from and losing other ways of transcendence while cultivating one way of transcendence."

Avalokiteshvara asked, "What is meant by inexpedient action?"

The Buddha replied, "When enlightening beings help people by means of the ways of transcendence, if they just give them material aid and consider that enough, failing to get them out of bad conditions and into good states, this is called inexpedient action. Why? Just doing this for people is not to be called truly helping them.

"It is like the case of dung. Be it much or little, nothing can make it fragrant and clean. In the same way, because of the pain that is due to transience, living beings are suffering by nature;

there is no expedient but to help them out with the entangling forms of material goods so as to enable them to become comfortable. But only haven in the sublime truth can be called the foremost benefit."

The enlightening being Avalokiteshvara also asked the Buddha, "How many purities do all the transcendent ways have?"

"The Buddha replied, "I have never said that the transcendent ways have any other purities besides the aforementioned five aspects. I will speak of the aspects of purity of the transcendent ways, however, based on these matters, in general and in particular.

"In general, the aspects of purity of all the transcendent ways are seven in number. First, enlightening beings do not seek to be known to others for these practices. Second, once they have seen these practices, they do not become partisans or fanatics. Third, they do not entertain doubts about these practices, such as whether or not one can actually attain great enlightenment thereby. Fourth, they never praise themselves, slander others, or slight anyone. Fifth, they are never proud and indulgent. Sixth, they never consider a little attainment to be enough. Seventh, they do not become jealous of others on account of these practices.

"As for the aspects of purity of all the transcendent ways individually, these are also seven in number; that is, enlightening beings practice in accord with the seven characteristics of purity of giving as I teach. First, they practice pure giving through purity of gift. Second, they practice pure giving through purity of conduct. Third, they practice pure giving through purity of vision. Fourth, they practice pure giving through purity of mind. Fifth, they practice pure giving through purity of speech. Sixth, they practice pure giving through purity of knowledge. Seventh, they practice pure giving through purification of defilements. These are called the seven kinds of purity of giving.

"Enlightening beings can also understand all the points to be learned in the established rules of conduct. They can understand how to avoid transgression and how to be complete with constant discipline, stable discipline, consciously performed discipline, subconsciously operative discipline. They can understand how to take in and study all points to be learned. These are called the seven purities of discipline.

"Suppose enlightening beings have deep faith when the results of their actions variously develop, and do not get upset when anything unfavorable occurs, and do not holler back or get angry or violent, do not have recourse to fear or humiliation, do not retaliate in any way, do not hold grudges, are not angered by admonition, and do not wait for others to admonish them. They do not practice forbearance with a mind emotionally affected by fear, and they do not give it up because of favor. These are called the seven kinds of purity of forbearance.

"Suppose enlightening beings realize the equal nature of diligence, and neither elevate themselves nor look down on others because of their own great diligence, are imbued with great strength and great energy, are capable, steadfast and vigorous, and do not abandon good ways. These are called the seven kinds of purity of diligence.

"Suppose enlightening beings have attained concentration and meditation with perfect comprehension of forms, full concentration and meditation, complete concentration and meditation, progressive concentration and meditation, independent concentration and meditation, well-cultivated concentration and meditation, and infinite concentration and meditation, through learning from the canon of enlightening beings; these are called the seven kinds of purity of meditation.

"If enlightening beings avoid the two extremes of affirmation and denial, and travel the middle path, that is called insight. By this insight, they truly know the meaning of the doors of liberation, the doors of liberation that are emptiness, wishlessness, and signlessness. They truly know the meaning of having inherent nature, referring to conceptualized nature, dependent nature, or true nature. They truly know the meaning of having no inherent nature, referring to the essencelessness of appearances, origination, and ultimate truth. They truly know conventional truth, referring to the five fields of knowledge. They truly know the ultimate truth, referring to seven suchnesses, or seven kinds of thusness. They also dwell much on one pure principle beyond all descriptions without discrimination; the immeasurable totality of truths is the focus, and by observation they can accomplish the practice of the teachings and their auxiliaries. These are called the seven kinds of purity of insight."

Avalokiteshvara then asked, "What functions does each of the five aspects you mentioned have?"

The Buddha replied, "Those aspects have five functions. Because of having no defiling habits, there being no polluting influence or clinging, enlightening beings in the present state are always seriously and diligently engaged in the transcendent ways they are practicing, without any negligence. Because of having no attachment, they internalize the cause of future alertness. Because of having no fault, they can correctly practice the transcendent ways to supremely good fulfillment, supremely good clarity, and supremely good purity. Because of having no discrimination, by skill in means the transcendent ways are soon fulfilled. Because of proper dedication, wherever one may be, the transcendent ways and their pleasant fruits will all be boundless, up to supreme perfect enlightenment."

Avalokiteshvara then asked, "Of the transcendent ways thus explained, what aspect is greatest, what is undefiled, what is most brilliant, what is immovable, what is most pure?"

The Buddha replied, "The natures of having no defiling habits, no attachment, and proper dedication are greatest. The natures of impeccability and nondiscrimination, and absence of action with tainted judgment, are most brilliant. Having entered the stage of nonregression is called immovable. If the ten stages take in Buddhahood, this inclusion is most pure."

Avalokiteshvara also asked, "Why are the pleasant fruits and developments of the transcendent ways that enlightening beings attain perpetual and inexhaustible? And why are the transcendent ways inexhaustible too?"

The Buddha replied, "Because they progressively develop cooperatively as the enlightening beings practice them uninterruptedly."

Avalokiteshvara asked, "Why do the enlightening beings deeply believe in the transcendent ways and have enthusiasm for them, rather than the pleasant fruits of the transcendent ways?"

The Buddha replied, "There are five reasons. First, the transcendent ways are the cause of supreme joy and bliss. Second, the transcendent ways are the cause of ultimate benefit for everyone, oneself and others included. Third, the transcendent ways are the cause of pleasant rewards in the future. Fourth, the transcendent ways are not a basis for defilements. Fifth, the transcendent ways are not things that ultimately change and perish."

Avalokiteshvara asked, "How many kinds of supreme power does each of the transcendent ways have?"

The Buddha replied, "Each one has four. First, when correctly practicing these transcendent ways, one is able to abandon envy, bad conduct, anger, laziness, distraction, and opinionated tendencies. Second, when correctly practicing these transcendent ways, one can make them true sustenance for supreme perfect enlightenment. Third, when correctly practicing these transcendent ways, one can absorb them into oneself and benefit others thereby. When correctly practicing these transcendent ways, one will be able to attain great endless pleasant rewards in the future."

Avalokiteshvara asked, "What is the cause of these transcendent ways? What is the effect? What is the benefit?"

The Buddha replied, "All these transcendent ways have great compassion as their cause. Subtle, pleasant fruits benefiting all sentient beings are the effect. Complete unexcelled great enlightenment is the great benefit."

Avalokiteshvara asked, "If enlightening beings have endless wealth and have developed great compassion, why is there still poverty to be found among people?"

The Buddha replied, "This is due to people's own errors in action. Enlightening beings are always altruistic and always have endless wealth and treasure; if there were no evildoing on the part of people themselves to form a barrier, how could poverty be found in the world? Such people are like hungry ghosts oppressed by great heat and thirst who see the ocean as all dried up; it is not the fault of the ocean, but of their own deeds. In the same way, the wealth given away by enlightening beings is like the ocean, without any flaw, but there is error on the part of people's own actions, like the power of the evil deeds of hungry ghosts, which causes there to be no water."

Avalokiteshvara asked, "By what transcendent way is the essencelessness of all things apprehended?"

The Buddha replied, "You can apprehend the essencelessness of things by transcendent insight."

Avalokiteshvara asked, "If transcendent insight can apprehend the essencelessness of things, why does it not apprehend having an essence?"

The Buddha replied, "I have never said that essencelessness is apprehended by essencelessness. Essencelessness is beyond words, inwardly realized, but cannot be explained without words. Therefore I say that transcendent insight can apprehend the essencelessness of things."

Avalokiteshvara asked, "What are the ways of transcendence, the near-transcendent ways, and the great transcendent ways of which you speak?"

The Buddha replied, "If enlightening beings spend measureless time practicing giving and so on, and they develop good qualities, but yet their afflictions are still active and they are as yet unable to master them but are mastered by them, this is referred to as the operation of devotion in the warming-up phase of the stage of devoted practice. At this time, they are called ways of transcendence.

"If enlightening beings practice giving and the rest of the ways for measureless time and gradually develop more perfectly accomplished good qualities, yet their afflictions are still active, but they can master them and are not mastered by them, this refers to the first stage up, and these are called near-transcendent ways.

"If enlightening beings practice giving and the rest of the ways for measureless time further and perfect good qualities even more, so that no afflictions are active, which occurs from the eighth stage up, these are called great transcendent ways."

Avalokiteshvara asked, "How many kinds of stupefaction from afflictions can occur in these stages?"

The Buddha replied, "In brief, there are three. First are stupefactions that lose their partners. This occurs in the first five stages. Why? Active expressions of noncongenital afflictions are partners of the active expressions of congenital afflictions; since they cease to exist during that time, they are called stupefactions that lose their partners.

"Second are weak stupefactions. This refers to the minute active expressions of afflictions in the sixth and seventh stages, because they will not be expressed in action if you practice quelling them.

"Third are subtle stupefactions. This refers to the eighth stage up, where afflictions are not actively expressed, but there is still the barrier of knowledge as a basis."

Avalokiteshvara asked, "By ending how many kinds of gross materialism are these stupefactions revealed?"

The Buddha replied, "Just two kinds. The first two are revealed by ending gross materialism in the skin; the third is revealed by ending gross materialism in the flesh. If one ends gross materialism in the bones, I say that one has forever left the realm of stupefaction and is in the stage of Buddhahood."

Avalokiteshvara asked, "How many incalculable eons does it take to end this kind of grossness?"

The Buddha replied, "Three incalculable eons, or infinite eons. That is because the eons in the years, months, fortnights, days, nights, hours, minutes, seconds, and moments cannot be counted."

Avalokiteshvara asked, "What are the characteristics, what are the faults, what are the merits of the afflictions aroused by enlightening beings in each stage?"

The Buddha replied, "The characteristic is nondefiling. Why? The enlightening beings have certainly understood the spiritual realm of all principles in the first stage, and so they must arouse afflictions knowingly, not because of ignorance. Therefore the characteristic of the afflictions is said to be nondefiling. Because the afflictions cannot cause pain to the enlightening beings themselves, they have no fault. Enlightening beings arouse such afflictions as will be able to stop the causes of suffering among sentient beings; therefore they have immeasurable merits."

Avalokiteshvara said, "It is wonderful how great the virtues and benefits of supreme enlightenment are, that enlightening beings may arouse afflictions and yet surpass the goodness of all people and individual saints, to say nothing of their other countless virtues."

Avalokiteshvara also asked the Buddha, "You say the vehicle of disciples and the great vehicle are just one vehicle. What is the secret meaning behind this?"

The Buddha replied, "In the vehicle of disciples, I explain the nature of various things, such as the five clusters, the inner six sense faculties, the outer six sense data, and so on. In the great vehicle, I say those things are one and the same reality realm, with one and the same innermost meaning. Therefore I do not say the vehicles are different.

"Yet there may be those who develop a mistaken notion of the meaning according to the words, so that one vehicle is aggrandized and one is diminished. Such people also think the different principles of the vehicles are mutually contradictory, and they argue among themselves more and more. That is the secret meaning behind this."

Then, to recapitulate, the Buddha spoke these verses:

The contents of the stages, and what is to be cured,
Higher developments, undertakings, and learning:
Cultivating the will based on the great vehicle
Expounded by Buddha results in great awakening.
I explain the variety of phenomena,
And also say their innermost meaning is one,
Whether in lower or higher vehicle;
So I say the vehicles have no difference.
If you make up false literalist notions of the meaning,
Aggrandizing or diminishing,
Saying the greater and lesser vehicles are opposed,
This ignorant interpretation produces conflict.

Then the enlightening being Avalokiteshvara asked the Buddha, "Within this teaching of unraveling of mysteries, what should this teaching be called? How should I uphold it?"

The Buddha replied, "This is called the definitive teaching of the transcendent ways of the stages, and you should uphold this teaching of the definitive meaning of the transcendent ways of the stages of enlightening beings."

When this teaching was spoken, there were seventy-five thousand enlightening beings in the audience who attained absorption in the light of the great vehicle of enlightening beings.

8. DEEDS OF THE ENLIGHTENED

Then the great enlightening beings Manjushri, the Glorious One, said to the Buddha, "You speak of the reality body of the enlightened, who have arrived at thusness. What are the characteristics of the reality body?"

The Buddha said, "Thoroughly cultivating the transcendent ways in the stages of enlightening, attaining emancipation, transformation of the mental basis, and completion—these are called characteristics of the reality body of the enlightened.

"These characteristics are inconceivable for two reasons; because of absence of false conceptions and because nothing is fabricated. And yet people think up false conceptions of something created, and cling to them."

Manjushri asked, "Is the transformation of the mental basis that is attained by hearers and individual illuminates called the reality body?"

The Buddha said, "No."

Manjushri asked, "What body is it called?"

The Buddha replied, "The body of liberation. All hearers and individual illuminates are said to be equal to the Buddhas in terms of the body of liberation. In terms of the reality body, they are said to be different. The reality body of Buddhas is different, by the most excellent difference of infinite qualities, which are beyond counting, or even approximation by simile."

Manjushri also asked the Buddha, "How should we know the characteristics of the origination of the enlightened?"

The Buddha replied, "The works of the emanated bodies of all Buddhas are like the world producing all species. The characteristics thereof are adornment and maintenance by the myriad qualities of the enlightened. You should realize that the characteristics of the emanated body have origination, but the characteristics of the reality body have no origination."

Manjushri asked, "How should we know the skill in means of manifesting emanated bodies?"

The Buddha replied, "Being conceived simultaneously in a royal or noble family in all Buddha-lands in all universes, being born, growing up, experiencing pleasures, leaving home, sharing ascetic practices, giving up ascetic practices, and attaining true enlightenment are manifested in succession. This is called the Buddhas' skill in means of manifesting emanated bodies."

Manjushri asked, "How many kinds of different speech sounds are held by the body of all Buddhas, by which words the immature people they teach are matured, while those who are already mature quickly attain liberation by focusing on them?"

The Buddha replied, "There are three kinds of words of Buddhas. One kind is scripture. Second is discipline. Third is the mother."

Manjushri asked, "What are scripture, discipline, and the mother?"

The Buddha replied, "When I reveal teachings regarding what is so, based on what will help people, this is called scripture. This may be based on four things, on nine things, or on twenty-nine things.

"What are the four things? First is listening. Second is taking it to heart. Third is putting it into practice. Fourth is enlightenment.

"What are the nine things? Defining people, defining their experience, defining their origin, defining their life after birth, defining their defilement and purity, defining their differences, defining the explainer, defining the explained, defining the assemblies.

"What are the twenty-nine things? Based on contamination, there are ingrained actions. These go on one after another. Then one thinks of this as a person, and this becomes a cause of future routines. Conceiving notions of phenomena, these become a cause of future routines. Based on what is pure, there is focus on objects of meditation. One then works diligently on this. The mind is then at peace. One experiences well-being in the present life. There are techniques of transcending all causes of misery. There are three ways of knowing these thoroughly: based on thorough knowledge of error; based on thorough knowledge of wrong actions; based on thorough knowledge of inner removal of conceit. Practicing these bases leads to experience of realization; cultivation leads to stabilization. There are appropriate modes of practice for that, with appropriate points of focus. This involves skill in observing what has been stopped and what has not, skill in observing confusion and distraction, ability to avoid confusion and distraction, and knowledge of the basis of nondistraction. There is intense application of effort in practice, leading to the benefits of practice, which produce steadfastness, embodiment of sagacious conduct, and embodiment of the accompaniments of sagacious conduct. Ultimately there is arrival at reality, realization of nirvana, and correct insight into the world through proper guidance, the peak of correct insight, beyond that attained by all outsiders. There is also regression caused by not practicing this, regression that is so called because of not practicing the right teaching, not because of a fault in the insight.

"The indications of specific proscriptions and the rules associated with specific proscriptions applying to disciples and enlightening beings are called discipline."

Manjushri asked, "How many aspects of the specific prohibitions for enlightening beings are there?"

The Buddha replied, "There are seven. First is explaining the guidelines to be accepted. Second is explaining the advantages of following them. Third is explaining things that tend toward transgression. Fourth is explaining the nature of transgression. Fifth is explaining the nature of nontransgression. Sixth is explaining how to get away from transgression. Seventh is explaining the relinquishment of rules of behavior."

The Buddha continued, "When I define, analyze, and illustrate things in terms of eleven kinds of characteristics, this is called the mother. What are these eleven kinds of characteristics? The first kind is the characteristics of mundane convention. The second kind is the characteristics of ultimate truth. The third kind is the characteristics of the points of focus of the elements of enlightenment. The fourth kind is the characteristics of practice. The fifth kind is the characteristics of identity. The sixth kind is the characteristics of effects. The seventh kind is the characteristics of reception of teaching. The eighth kind is the characteristics of obstacles to the teaching. The ninth kind is characteristics of accord with the teaching. The tenth kind is characteristics of ills. The eleventh kind is characteristics of benefits attained.

"There are three kinds of characteristics of mundane convention. First is speaking in terms of personality. Second is speaking in terms of conceptualized identities. Third is speaking in terms of the functions of phenomena.

"The characteristics of ultimate truth refer to the seven suchnesses, or seven kinds of thusness.

"The characteristics of the points of focus of the elements of enlightenment refer to all kinds of objects of knowledge.

"The characteristics of practice refer to eight practices of contemplation: contemplation of real truth, contemplation of construction, contemplation of faults, contemplation of virtues, contemplation of principles, contemplation of routines, contemplation of reason, and contemplation of totality and distinction.

"Real truth means the true thusness of all things.

"Construction means setting up the personality, or setting up the conceptualized identities of things, or setting up all-embracing answers, particularized answers, answers made after returning a question, and answering by not answering, or setting up the difference between covert and overt predictions of enlightenment.

"Faults refer to the various defiled states of which I speak, which have innumerable different ills.

"Virtues refer to the various pure states of which I speak, which have innumerable different benefits.

"Principles are of six kinds: principles of true meaning, principles of realization, principles of teaching and guidance, principles of avoiding extremes, principles of inconceivability, and principles of intended meaning.

"Routines refer to the becoming, subsistence, and decay of what is created in past, present, and future, as well as the causal conditions, successive conditions, conditioning conditions, and dominant conditions.

"Reason is of four kinds: the reason of relativity, the reason of function, the reason of realization, and the reason of natural law.

"The reason of relativity means the causes or conditions by which one can produce practices and corresponding explanations.

"The reason of function means the causes or conditions by which one can apprehend things, or deal with them, or put them to use once they have arisen.

"The reason of realization means the causes or conditions by which one can establish the principles that have been set up, explained, and proposed so as to effect correct awakening.

"This latter reason is also of two general kinds, pure and impure. It is called pure based on five characteristics, and called impure based on seven characteristics.

"What are the five characteristics based on which it is called pure? First is apprehension by direct witness. Second is apprehension based on direct witness. Third is deduction by analogy. Fourth is complete truthfulness. Fifth is true purity of teaching.

"Apprehension by direct witness refers to the impermanence of all conditioned things, the suffering inherent in all conditioned states, and the identitylessness, or selflessness, of all phenomena. These are apprehended by direct experience in the world. This sort of thing is called that which is apprehended by direct witness.

"That which is apprehended based on direct witness refers to such things as the instantaneousness of all that happens, the existence of other worlds, and the nondisappearance of pure and impure deeds. Those things which cannot be actually seen but can be deduced are said to be apprehended based on direct witness, because they can be seen by way of crude impermanence, because the various differences in people can be found to be due to their various actions, and because it can be found that the happiness or misery of people is based on their pure or impure deeds.

"That which is deduced by analogy means drawing on birth and death, which are common knowledge, from among the assemblages of inner and outer patterns, drawing on commonly known and experienced forms of lack of freedom as analogies, and drawing on commonly known and experienced external deterioration and growth as analogies.

"Complete truthfulness means positive ability to establish

what is affirmed, whether by direct witness, based on direct witness, or by analogy.

"The truly pure Teaching refers to what is said by the omniscient one, such as that nirvana is ultimate peace.

"Skillful examination of pure reason is so called on the basis of these five characteristics. Because it is pure, it should be put into practice."

Then Manjushri asked the Buddha, "How many characteristics of omni-science are there?"

The Buddha replied, "In brief, there are five. First is appearing in the world with the voice of all-knowledge and being heard everywhere. Second is perfection of the thirty-two marks of greatness. Third is attainment of the ten powers, with ability to cut off the doubts of all people. Fourth is attainment of the fourfold confidence in expounding the truth, unrefuted by any other arguments, able to refute all false arguments. Fifth is manifesting the attainability of the eightfold noble path and its fruits. Living in this way, cutting through the web of doubts, being irrefutable while able to refute others, manifesting attainment of the noble path—these five are called characteristics of omni-science.

"This reason of realization is called pure based on direct experience, inference, wise teaching, and the aforementioned characteristics.

"As for the seven characteristics that are called impure, the first is when other cases in the same category can be found. Second is when other cases in different categories can be found. Third is when everything can be found in the same category. Fourth is when everything can be found in different categories. Fifth is when an example is taken from a different category. Sixth is not being completely true. Seventh is not being pure teaching.

"If reference is made to all phenomena being essentially representations of consciousness, then it can be said that everything can be found in the same category.

"If reference is made to the different appearances, natures, functions, laws, causes, and effects, pursuing each of these different characteristics is certain to produce even more individually different characteristics. Then it can be said that everything can be found in different categories.

"If other cases can be found in the same category, or if an example applies to everything else as well, because of this the proposition is not established with certainty; this is called not being completely true.

"Also, if other cases can be found in different categories, or if an example applies to everything in the same category, because of this the proposition is not established with certainty, so it is said to be not completely true.

"Not being completely true, it is not well-examined, pure reason. Not being pure, it should not be practiced.

"If an example is taken from a different category, or if it is not pure teaching, know that neither the substance nor the essence is pure.

"The reason of natural law means that whether or not a Buddha appears in the world, the nature of reality remains unaffected; realities abide in the reality realm. This is called the reason of natural law.

"Totality and distinction refer to first generally expounding one statement of the teaching, then subsequently distinguishing and definitely revealing the differentiations in various statements.

"Characteristics of identity refer to the distinct elements by which it is possible to attain enlightenment, which I explain as involving practices and having conditions, such as the four points of mindfulness.

"Characteristics of effects refer to the extermination of mundane and transmundane afflictions, and to the resulting worldly and transcendental virtues developed.

"Characteristics of reception and teaching refer to reception by liberated intelligence and explaining for others.

"Characteristics of obstacles to the Teaching refer to polluting factors that can hinder the practice of the elements of enlightenment.

"Characteristics of accord with the Teaching refer to practices that accomplish a lot.

"Characteristics of ills refer to the faults in the factors that obstruct the Teaching.

"Characteristics of benefits refer to the virtues of following the Teaching."

Then the enlightening being Manjushri said to the Buddha, "Please give the enlightening beings a brief talk on concentrated formulations of scripture, discipline, and the mother, not common to outsiders, by which concentrated formulations enlightening beings are enabled to gain access to the deepest inner meanings of the teachings expounded by the enlightened."

The Buddha said to Manjushri, "Listen and I will give you a brief talk on the uncommon concentrated formulae that enable enlightening beings to gain understanding of the words I speak with hidden intent.

"I say that all things, be they polluted phenomena or pure phenomena, are totally void of function, and also void of personality. Because nothing has any connection to fabrication, it is not that polluted phenomena are impure at first, then later will be purified, and it is not that pure phenomena were purified after having first been polluted. Ordinary mortals cling to the distinctions in identities of personalities projected on phenomena in crude material bodies, and become stupefied by arbitrary views; because of these conditions, they conceive of the ideas of self and belongings. Due to these erroneous ideas, they think, 'I see, I hear, I smell, I taste, I feel, I know, I consume, I work, I am polluted, I am pure,' and misguided efforts of corresponding varieties go into operation.

"Any who can know this as it really is can then detach from the body of gross materiality forever and attain the ultimate purity in which no affliction remains, beyond all falsehood, based on noncontrivance, free from deliberate effort.

"This is a summary of the uncommon concentrated formulae."

Then the Buddha spoke a verse to recapitulate:

All phenomena, polluted and pure,
Are void of function and personality.
Following my teaching, detach from fabrication,
And polluted and pure things are neither before nor after.
Stupefied views of the gross material body
Condition ideas of self and possession;
Based on this, one wrongly imagines,
"I see, I eat, I am polluted or pure."
If one can know this as it really is,
One can detach forever from the gross body
And attain undefiled purity, beyond falsehood,
Based on noncontrivance, free from deliberate effort.

Then the enlightening being Manjushri asked the Buddha, "How should we know the characteristics of the arousal of a Buddha's mind?"

The Buddha replied, "Buddhahood is not manifested by mind, intellect, or consciousness. Nevertheless, the arising of mental events without deliberate effort does occur in Buddhas. You should know that these phenomena are like magical apparitions."

Manjushri asked, "If the reality body of Buddhas is beyond all deliberate effort, how can mental events occur without effort?"

The Buddha replied, "Arousal of mind occurs because of the

power of concerted action of technique and insight previously cultivated.

"For example, when one enters into mindless sleep, one does not make a deliberate effort to awaken; one awakens again by virtue of the power and momentum of previous engagement in action.

"It is also like being in extinct trance: one does not make a deliberate effort to arise from trance; one arises from trance by virtue of the power and momentum of previous engagement in action.

"Just as the mind is rearoused when coming out of deep sleep or extinct trance, in the same way mental events recur in Buddhas by virtue of the power of concerted actions of technique and insight previously cultivated."

Manjushri then asked the Buddha, "Should an emanation body of a Buddha be said to have a mind or to have no mind?"

The Buddha replied, "It neither has a mind nor has no mind. Why? Because of having no mind relative to self, and because of having a mind relative to others."

Manjushri then asked, "What is the difference between the sphere of the Buddhas and the realm of the Buddhas?"

The Buddha replied, "The sphere of the Buddhas refers to all kinds of pure domains of enlightenment adorned with infinite inconceivable qualities, common to all Buddhas.

"The realm of the Buddhas refers to all kinds of distinctions of five realms. What are the five? First is the realm of sentient beings. Second is the realm of worlds. Third is the realm of principle. Fourth is the realm of pacification. Fifth is the realm of expedient techniques of pacification.

"This is the distinction between the sphere and the realm of the Buddhas."

Then Manjushri asked the Buddha, "World Honored One, Buddhas attain true awakening, turn the wheel of true teaching, and enter ultimate nirvana; by what characteristics should these three things be known?"

The Buddha replied, "You should know that these three are all nondualistic. That means Buddhas neither attain true awakening nor do not attain true awakening, neither turn the wheel of true teaching nor do not turn the wheel of true teaching, neither enter ultimate nirvana nor do not enter ultimate nirvana. Why? Because the reality body of Buddhas is ultimately pure, and because the emanation bodies of Buddhas are always manifest."

Manjushri also asked the Buddha, "Sentient beings see, hear, and attend the emanation bodies only, whereby they develop virtues. What affinity has Buddha with them?"

The Buddha replied, "Their relationship with Buddha is the supreme object of focus for them; and the emanation body involved is maintained by the power of Buddha."

Then Manjushri asked, "If it is equanimous and effortless, how does the body of Buddha radiate the light of great knowledge and produce the images of countless emanation bodies for sentient beings? The body of liberation of hearers and individual illuminates does not have these things."

The Buddha replied, "It is like the light radiating equanimously and effortlessly from the sun and moon, or from water and fire crystals. Only water and fire crystals held by beings of great power can do this, not other water and fire crystals. So it is because of the influential power of the actions of sentient beings.

"It is also like imprints stamped from a jewel engraved by a skilled artisan. Imprints cannot come from other jewels, which are not engraved. In the same way, the reality body of Buddhas is put together by focus on the infinite techniques and insights of the realm of reality, cultivating them supremely well and polishing them to perfection; from this it is possible to radiate the light of great knowledge and produce the images of all sorts of emanation bodies. Such things do not come from the body of liberation alone."

Then Manjushri said to the Buddha, "As the World Honored One says, the power and support of Buddhas and enlightening beings enable people to be born in rich and noble families in the realm of desire, with personal and material fulfillment. Personal and material fulfillment in the heavens of the realm of desire, or the realms of form and formlessness, can also be attained. World Honored One, what is the inner meaning of this?"

The Buddha replied, "The power and support of Buddhas and enlightening beings, be it their ways or their practices, can enable people to attain personal and material fulfillment in all situations, in the sense that we explain to them such-and-such ways and practices according to their needs, so that any who correctly carry out these ways and practices will attain personal and material fulfillment in all situations.

If people violate these ways and practices and make light of them, and if they have a vicious and malevolent attitude toward me, then after their lives are ended, the bodies and material goods they will get wherever they are will be base and inferior.

"Manjushri, in view of these conditions, you should realize that the power and support of Buddhas and enlightening beings can not only make personal and material fulfillment possible; the support and power of Buddhas and enlightening beings can also make people's bodies and possessions base and inferior."

Manjushri then asked the Buddha, "World Honored One, in defiled lands, what things are easy to find, and what things are hard to find? In pure lands, what things are easy to find, and what things are hard to find?"

The Buddha replied, "In defiled lands, eight things are easy to find, while two things are hard to find.

"What are the eight things that are easy to find? First is false philosophies. Second is suffering sentient beings. Third is differences in race, caste, and family, and their flourishing and decline over the generations. Fourth is the currency of bad practices and evil acts. Fifth is repeated violation of ethics. Sixth is bad tendencies and miserable states. Seventh is lesser vehicles. Eighth is enlightening beings with inferior devotion and effort.

"What two things are hard to come by? One is an assembly of enlightening beings with higher devotion and intense effort. Second is the appearance of a Buddha in the world.

"In pure lands, the situation is reversed. The former eight things are very hard to find, while the latter two are easy to find."

Now Manjushri asked the Buddha, "Within this teaching explaining the deep mysteries, how should we name these instructions, and how should we follow them?"

The Buddha replied, "These are called instructions in the complete meaning of the deeds of the enlightened. You should follow them as instructions in the complete meaning of the deeds of the enlightened."

When these instructions in the complete meaning of the deeds of the enlightened were explained, seventy-five thousand advanced enlightening beings in the great assembly were able to attain conscious witness of the complete reality body.

NOTES

CHAPTER 2. CHARACTERISTICS OF ULTIMATE TRUTH

uncreated: Another name for nirvana in the objective, metaphysical sense of the ultimate emptiness and ungraspability of all phenomena.

discrimination: This word is used with two meanings. One meaning is negative: false discrimination, arbitrary thought. The other is positive: true discrimination, accurate discernment.

cessation and contemplation: Also called tranquillity and observation, this binome refers to the two basic aspects of meditation, *cessation* of arbitrary thinking and *contemplation* of objective truths.

clusters: The components of being: form (matter); sensation; conception; coordination; consciousness.

nourishment: The four kinds of nourishment are food, contact, thought, and consciousness.

elements: The eighteen elements are the six sense faculties, the six sense consciousnesses, and the six sense fields.

points of mindfulness: In the elementary stage of practice, these refer to mindfulness of the body as impure, sensation as irritating, mind as fickle, and phenomena as impermanent. After attainment of nirvana, the practice shifts to mindfulness of the body as like space, of sensation as neither internal nor external, of mind as ungraspable, and of phenomena as neither good nor bad.

right efforts: The efforts to stop what is bad, to prevent future evil, to promote existing good, and to foster further good.

base of occult powers: Intent, will, energy, and reflection.

religious faculties and powers: Faith, energy, recollection, concentration, intelligence; these five faculties, when developed, become the five powers.

branches of enlightenment: Discernment, energy, joy, lightness, recollection, concentration, nonattachment.

eightfold noble path: Right seeing, thinking, speaking, working, living, diligence, recollection, and concentration; a traditional formulation of the way to emancipation, attributed to the Buddha.

CHAPTER 4. CHARACTERISTICS OF ALL PHENOMENA

afflictions: The six major afflictions are greed, hatred, ignorance, conceit, opinionatedness, and suspicion.

repetitious cycles: Samsara, the working out of routine habits of thought, word, and deed.

vehicle of sainthood: Principles and practices leading to subjective nirvana, the aim being to attain perfect inner peace.

vehicle of self-enlightenment: Principles and practices for individual realization of ultimate truth, the aim being to transcend the conditioned world by one's own efforts.

vehicle of universal enlightenment: Principles and practices of collective evolution through individual and group development, the aim being to foster both the worldly and transcendental welfare of all beings.

disciples: Followers of the vehicle of sainthood.

behavioral obstruction: Problems and impediments caused by actions; blockage created by behavior that is not in harmony with reality.

twelve sense media: The six senses and their respective data fields.

twelve elements of becoming: Ignorance, activity, consciousness, name and form, six senses, contact, sensation, craving, grasping, becoming, birth, aging, and dying.

noble truths (or holy truths): The truth of suffering, the truth of the cause of suffering, the truth of the end of suffering, the truth of the way to end suffering.

great vehicle: Another general name for the vehicle of universal enlightenment.

acceptance of nonorigination: Peace attained by acquiescence to the ultimate ungraspability of the essence of phenomena. See *The Flower Ornament Scripture,* book 29, "The Ten Acceptances."

CHAPTER 6. ANALYZING YOGA

eight stages of meditation: Successive stages of meditation concentration, characterized by the following elements:

1. consideration, examination, joy, bliss, singlemindedness
2. inner purity, joy, bliss, singlemindedness
3. equanimity, recollection, insight, bliss, singlemindedness
4. neither pain nor pleasure, equanimity, recollection, singlemindedness
5. absorption in the infinity of space
6. absorption in infinite consciousness
7. absorption in infinite nothingness
8. neither perception nor nonperception

transformation of the mind basis: Changing the basis of consciousness from afflictions to enlightenment. *Transformation of the mental basis* means that mind no longer leans on its own projections and representations as grounding in objective reality.

scriptures: Sutras, or discourses of Buddha.

treatises: shastras, or texts written by ancient Buddhist doctors to elucidate and interpret the teachings found in the sutra-scriptures.

hearers: Followers of the vehicle of sainthood.

CHAPTER 7. THE TRANSCENDENT WAYS OF THE STAGES

tranquillity and observation These terms, referring to the basic complementary modal techniques of meditation, are also rendered *stopping and seeing* or *cessation and contemplation*.

the uninterrupted mind This refers to the underlying continuum of mind subtending mental images. Realizing that images are only mind, one can cease conceptualizing them as independent external entities, and can thus contemplate them as "such," without internally talking about them.

ten stages of enlightenment: For a detailed account of the ten major stages of enlightenment, see *The Flower Ornament Scripture,* book 26.

emptiness: For a detailed treatment of "emptiness," see *The Flower Ornament Scripture* pp. 748–749 and 870–876 (in the 1986 edition of vol. 2, pp. 60–61 and 182–188).

emptiness of appearances: This means that subjective representations or descriptions of reality are empty of objective substance.

emptiness of nonsuccession: This means that the cognitive continuity of phenomena depends on repetition of specific cognitive habits; when these habits are broken, the apparent continuity is broken.

emptiness of ungraspability: Phenomena cannot be apprehended in themselves, but only in relation to a perceiver and a perceptual context. Therefore the "thing in itself" is ungraspable to the conceiving mind and thus is "empty" of the putative characteristics by which cognition and imagination try to "grasp" it.

emptiness of inherent nature: No thing exists independently, in and of itself, but a thing exists only as a product of causes, and in relation to everything upon which it depends and by which it is conditioned; therefore phenomena are said to be void of inherent nature.

ultimate emptiness: The reality of phenomena is ultimately empty of solid attributes as imagined by the conceptual faculty of subjective consciousness.

emptiness of essencelessness: Phenomena are said to be empty of essence in that they have no absolute existence of their own.

emptiness of ultimate truth: The truth of things is that they are ultimately innocent of what we subjectively imagine about them.

being satisfied with a little In this context, this expression refers to spiritual understanding, not material goods.

five veils There are somewhat different lists of these veils, according to particular schools. This scripture has doubt and wrong action as one veil, oblivion and sleepiness as another, added to the three veils of doubt, craving, and resentment. Another classical list of the five veils is craving, resentment, drowsiness, excitement, and doubt.

the barrier of knowledge: Knowledge is a barrier to the extent that it mesmerizes the subjective mind into subconsciously presuming that there is nothing more than what it knows.

liberations / points of dominance / points of totality: The "eight liberations" are the results of eight purification procedures known as the eight rejections. First is observation of external form while having ideas of form within. Second is observation of external form without any ideas of form within. Third is focus on purity. Fourth is focus on infinite space. Fifth is focus on infinite consciousness. Sixth is focus on nothingness. Seventh is focus on neither perception nor nonperception. Eighth is extinction of all sensation and perception.

The eight points of dominance are exercises in free manipulation of perception. The first involves viewing one's body as a corpse, then seeing the flesh fall away, until one sees one's own body as a bleached skeleton, shining with light. The second involves extending this practice to the world at large. The third involves observing one's own body with no conception of form. The fourth involves extending this practice to the world at large. The fifth involves absorption in the color blue. The sixth involves absorption in the color yellow. The seventh involves absorption in the color red. The eighth involves absorption in white.

The ten points of totality are exercises in absorption in the following points of attention: blue, yellow, red, white, earth, water, fire, air, space, consciousness.

Printed in the United States
by Baker & Taylor Publisher Services